Contents

Classroom Management for Meeting Individual Needs

At the beginning of the school year, you've probably experienced the great feeling most teachers share. You're ready and excited about a new group of students and know you'll be delighted by how uniquely individual they are. As the year unfolds, you'll focus on your students' levels of ability and the content they all need to learn; additionally, you must address the increasing demands made on your schedule.

If your classroom is typical, you have a variety of students, including those who receive special services through Title I and special education. Most likely, you also have students who need to be challenged regularly. There are also increasing numbers of English language learners who need support and specialized teaching. You may have a combination classroom, but certainly you have students who just need good teaching, encouragement, and assistance during lessons and practice time.

Universal Access

Houghton Mifflin Reading: A Legacy of Literature includes a wealth of resources for universal access—that is, for helping all students achieve grade-level expectations. These resources include the *Handbook for English Language Learners, Extra Support Handbook,* and *Challenge Handbook*. For on-level students and for the groups you are not instructing, this handbook (the *Classroom Management Handbook*) provides independent activities and ties them to the selections, skills, and instruction in the *Houghton Mifflin Reading* curriculum. The activities provide a range of levels and interests for students. *Challenge Handbook* activities are week-long projects or shorter activities. In general, they bring students to higher levels of thinking, and they encourage flexible thinking and problem solving. They are designed for small group, partner, or individual work.

The *Classroom Management Handbook* and the group of universal access handbooks are to be used in addition to the core instruction in *Houghton Mifflin Reading*. Your Teacher's Edition also includes universal access support for students in a variety of ways:

- Literature for a range of ability levels
- Support for meeting individual needs at the beginning of each selection
- Options for challenge or extension, along with cross-curricular and writing activities in the Theme Resources sections
- Reading cards for grouping support
- Responding options for a wide range of levels and learning styles
- Reader's Library, which includes easier text connected by topic and skills to the main anthology selections

Houghton Mifflin Reading: A Legacy of Literacy *and this handbook will help you manage your classroom effectively so that you and all of your students can succeed.*

Classroom Management Solutions

Structure and resources, both for short-term and long-term management solutions, will help you maintain the best possible learning environment for your students. In this handbook, management planning is built in, and the scope and quality of activities and teacher support will make it possible to focus on *teaching*.

In this handbook:

- Flexible groups and **differentiated instruction** are thoroughly explained.
- You'll have a **five-step plan** to put into practice for ensuring that students can work independently.
- **Time management** guidance that's invaluable is included throughout.
- Helpful classroom **management tips** are provided.
- Each selection from the anthology has **assignment planning for independent work.**
- Each selection has a variety of **meaningful activities** and every activity has **teacher support**.
- Sources from *Houghton Mifflin Reading* are cited for **additional independent work.**

In the Walkthrough on pages xiv–xvii, the parts of the assignment planners and the independent activity pages are described. Each planner corresponds to the Daily Lesson Plans in your *Houghton Mifflin Reading* Teacher's Edition and organizes all the program materials you need both for group instruction and for independent assignments. The sections that follow—"Effective Classroom Management," "Five Steps to Independence," "Time Management and Other Tips"—provide grouping information and useful ideas for frequent reference.

EFFECTIVE CLASSROOM MANAGEMENT

Does this scenario sound familiar to you?

> *Just as you get started working with a small group, you must stop teaching to take care of other students who are off task. Once you get those students going again, you realize you've lost the attention of the group you were teaching!*

For many teachers, this cycle repeats itself throughout the day. By the end of the day, they are exhausted, but determined to do better. It is possible to meet students' literacy needs while keeping others engaged in independent projects and activities. Determination helps, along with patience and a plan.

In the past, teachers grouped students according to their reading abilities (e.g., "Robins, Bluebirds, and Sparrows"). Research has demonstrated that in ability groups, less experienced and low-achieving readers may not make adequate progress. In more recent years, reading became a whole class activity, but presented this challenge: For some students the pacing and instruction was too easy and slow, whereas for others it was too difficult and fast. It made sense, then, to mix whole class with smaller groups. Here's a quick review of some familiar instructional groups.

	Benefits	Limitations
Whole Class	Efficient for assigning work. All students hear the assignment. Creates community.	Not all student needs can be met. Attention levels vary. Unclear whether all students understand.
Cooperative	Learners take responsibility for their work. Social skills can be fostered. The work is focused.	One student may get all of the responsibility. Social interactions in the group may not work.
Special Group	Teacher can adjust pacing and fit assignment to learning style. Focused work is a better assessment opportunity.	Students take less responsibility. May engender a negative self-image if group is for slower learners, for example. Usually not enough time for separate group work.
Partners	Fosters 50–50 sharing. Work is independent of the teacher. Each student must participate.	Students can get distracted and off task. They may only work with a friend. Lack of group pressure.
Individual	Self-paced learning can build self-awareness. Students can also self-assess.	Assignments may not meet needs. May result in boredom or disengagement. Cannot learn from others.

To ensure that all students progress satisfactorily, more and more teachers are presently combining whole class instruction with small, flexible groups—*flexible* meaning that students' group membership is not constant. In essence, students do not stay in the same groups. Participation in groups depends on students' assessed literacy needs and strengths, other academic abilities, leadership skills, and the purpose for the group or whole class activity.

Differentiated Instruction Through Flexible Grouping

Educators use the term *differentiated instruction* to describe the practice of grouping students for specific reading and language arts activities and then moving them into different groups according to particular lessons. Teachers select and use instructional approaches and materials according to the academic strengths and needs of students.

Differentiated instruction also refers to meeting the social, emotional, and psychological needs of students so that they can develop independence, confidence, and the ability to work with others. Students must learn to work in small groups, with partners, and alone without your direct and constant attention. You provide an adequate amount of supervision, but your students work on their own, allowing you to focus your attention on teaching one group of students at a time with little or no interruption.

Instructional and Interactive Groups

There are a number of grouping options—more than listed in the chart on page iv, but it is helpful to think in terms of two categories: teacher-led (instructional) or independent (interactive). **Instructional groups** are those for whom you take a major role in providing direct instruction to a small group of students or the whole class. **Interactive groups** are less formal and meet throughout the day. Students in interactive groups are expected to complete work independently, with partners, or in small groups.

Instructional	Interactive
Using instruction in the Extra Support, Challenge, or ELL handbooks, or in the Teacher's Edition	*Using activities in Classroom Management Handbook, Challenge Handbook, or in the Teacher's Edition*
Instructional reading groups: These are homogeneous groups selected according to students' reading levels and needs. You directly teach story concepts, vocabulary, and comprehension, for example, using the Teacher's Edition or lessons in the handbooks.	**Partners/triads:** You informally ask students to: • work with a partner (or triad) • buddy-read for fluency practice • read self-selected materials independently • practice spelling words • peer-edit writing, and so forth.
Whole class lessons: You teach skills and strategy lessons from the Teacher's Edition to the whole class; also included are your daily routines and teacher read-alouds.	**Small groups:** You may assign table groups, such as "four-heads-in-the middle" groups, to accomplish a task such as brainstorming or clustering ideas.
Acceleration: You provide challenging instruction for advanced learners in above-grade-level texts. (See the *Challenge Handbook*.)	**Discussion circles:** In circle groups, students engage in discussions of stories or articles they've read, reciprocal teaching, or other discussion opportunities that don't require your explicit instruction. You may supply questions or guidelines to help them focus their conversations.
Preteaching: You prepare a small group of students for a whole class lesson that will follow. (See the *Extra Support Handbook* and the *Handbook for English Language Learners*.)	**Cooperative learning groups, centers**: Students are purposefully grouped to work together over time to complete an assignment or a project.
Reteach/Review: You work with a small group of struggling readers to reteach and review what has been previously taught. (See the *Extra Support Handbook* and the *Handbook for English Language Learners*.)	**Research:** Students in these groups are often accelerated learners who can do independent research in the classroom, on the Internet, or in the library.

Small, flexible instructional groups are better for students who need more support. Interactive groups work for those who are able to take what they have learned and apply it on their own, either with a partner or small group.

You may wish to pair or include other students with advanced or Challenge students who share similar interests and who may benefit from working with an accelerated learner. However, it's not ideal for Challenge students to be placed repeatedly in the role of tutor. Make it a goal to foster optimal achievement for advanced learners as well as for students who are struggling.

Through assessment and observation, you'll determine which students can benefit from Challenge instruction and which students need preteaching, reteaching, extra modeling, and practice with the content concepts you are teaching.

When you teach students to work together and independently, you are providing them with skills they will use the rest of their lives.

Five Steps to Independence

Unless your students can work independently and complete tasks on their own and with others, you'll have difficulty managing a variety of flexible groups. Independence won't happen by itself. You have to teach students how to work by themselves. This is a process that requires energy on your part, but the benefits add up.

1 Organize	2 Assess and Analyze	3 Teach	4 Practice	5 Evaluate
Get your classroom set up for independent work.	Think about the groups you need and who should be in them. Keep in mind that you'll rethink and regroup students regularly.	Invest in teaching students how to work with others.	Model how to complete independent activities.	Check your decisions and your students' efforts.

Step 1: Organize the Classroom for Independence

Take a look around your classroom. Do you have quiet areas where students can read or work alone, such as in a reading center or corner? Do you have areas for center work? Is there a special table where you can bring students together for Extra Support lessons or lessons for English language learners? Is there a special area where students can read and work with another student or "buddy?" In what places do you stand to teach the entire class? Can you and your students move to different areas of the room without disturbing anyone?

Consider various classroom configurations and think about which might work for your reading/language arts instructional block. Try to maximize the flow from one area to another with minimal confusion and disruption. Finally, post reminders to students about how to spend their time when they are not participating in instruction. Enlarge the "What I Can Do" poster (see the Classroom Management Masters at the back of this handbook) or create a version of your own.

Step 2: Determine Flexible Groups

Begin by assessing your students' reading and writing strengths and needs, interests, special talents, and language proficiencies (especially if they are English language learners). With *Houghton Mifflin Reading*, you have assessment opportunities at the theme level and selection level. Refer to the *Teacher's Assessment Handbook* for specific diagnostic information.

Use your assessment findings to guide the composition of groups. For instructional groups, group membership will vary depending on the lessons taught. For independent group work, think about who works well together and why. For Challenge projects and activities, you will need to designate group membership as carefully as you do other instructional groups.

Use 3 x 5 index cards, one for each student, to take notes on reading level, any reading frustrations, strengths you've noticed in subject areas or in interpersonal interactions, and other observations.

Student _____

Reading level _____

• academic strengths, leadership abilities

_____

• special management needs, if appropriate

_____

• linguistic needs (first and second language, if relevant)

_____

• noteworthy attendance patterns

_____

• choices of classmates with whom he or she would like to work

_____   _____

_____   _____

Sort the cards into groups, based on the purpose for each group. For example, some groups may be heterogeneous, in which you mix reading levels, leadership abilities, and varied language development. Other groups may be organized according to needs, resulting in homogeneous groups. Note on the back of the cards the groups students are in, to help monitor their progress over time and for conferencing with family members.

Electronic record keeping for creating reports based on daily observations is possible with the *Learner Profile*™ CD-ROM. Produced by Sunburst Technology and available with Houghton *Mifflin Reading*, *Learner Profile*™ lets you electronically record, manage, and report your assessment of student progress. Companion software *Learner Profile to Go*™ allows you to record student information on a handheld computer device.

When students are not working directly with you, they are expected to work quietly, collaboratively, and purposefully by themselves or with others.

Step 3: Teach Students How to Work with Others in Groups

Borrowing from cooperative learning research (Johnson & Johnson, 1972), assume that your students do not know how people in groups effectively work together. Before you place students in groups, talk with them about the social skills that are necessary for working with each other. You may find it helpful to do the following:

- Brainstorm with your students what they should do when they are working with other people in a group. Write the responses on the board, and include listening, taking turns, all participating, all staying on task, being nice to each other, supporting good ideas, finishing the task, and so forth.

- Complete a "Looks Like/Sounds Like/Feels Like" chart for social skills you feel are most important for your students' independent group work, such as listening, cooperating, staying on task, disagreeing appropriately, and so forth. Ask students to respond to each category. For example, "What does a group sound like if all group members are listening to each other?" "What does it feel like when others listen to you?" Record their responses. When a chart is complete, post it and refer to it often, especially in the beginning stages of group work.

Consider the benefits that independent group work will provide when you are able to teach your instructional groups with complete, focused attention.

GOOD LISTENING

Looks Like	Sounds Like	Feels Like
Everyone looking at the one who is speaking	Only one voice is heard	I feel good
Nodding heads	No one interrupts	It feels like my ideas have been heard
Leaning forward to hear		I feel my ideas are valued
Only one person's mouth is moving		I like that I hear how my ideas work or whether they need to be rethought
Everyone looks interested		

Step 4: Introduce, Model, and Provide Practice in How to Complete Independent Activities

Select and distribute a group activity from this handbook to all class members and explain how to complete the activity. Invite students to turn and work with two or three others sitting nearby. Monitor how well the groups are working by walking around and observing. Determine whether any off-task behaviors are management issues or whether the group members don't understand what to do. If it is the former, refer the group to relevant "Looks Like…" charts, reminding students of what they need to do while in a small group. If they're having difficulty with the activity, intervene and explain the directions again, modeling if necessary.

After every group has completed the task, lead a discussion, asking "What worked well? What did you have trouble with?" Let everyone participate in the discussion, remembering that your purpose is to assist students in learning about group dynamics and independence.

On the following day, divide students into interactive groups and remind everyone of the social skills needed for small group work. Introduce another independent activity intended for small groups. Be sure everyone has the appropriate materials and is ready to begin. At this point, tell your students that you will be pretending to work with a small group at your instructional group table. Have students begin working in their groups on the activity. Go to your table and busy yourself, only looking up if there is a serious problem. Show your students that you expect them to work together independently.

After about 10-15 minutes (or when students have completed the activity), debrief once again and praise positive group work. Revisit appropriate group behavior and discuss the pride people feel when they have completed a task on their own.

On a subsequent day, call an instructional group together at your work table. Have the rest of the students work in groups on a simple activity such as finding vocabulary words in anthology stories. Establish what everyone is to do and then teach your group. When an interactive group has problems, wait until after your lesson to discuss the difficulties they had (unless there is a safety issue). Debrief a final time.

Step 5: Evaluate the Independence of the Interactive Groups

After groups have worked together on an assigned activity for several sessions, have them complete a Group Work Form to encourage reflectivity, group cohesiveness, accountability, and responsibility. (See the Classroom Management Masters located at the back of this handbook.) Add this information to your evaluation of your groups when you determine whether to change the membership of groups or whether there are aspects of group work that need specific attention, such as transitioning from large to small groups, for example.

You may also wish to monitor students' developing independent skills with the blackline master checklist at the back of this handbook (Checklist for Assessing Independence). This may be helpful when conferencing with your students as well as with their parents or guardians.

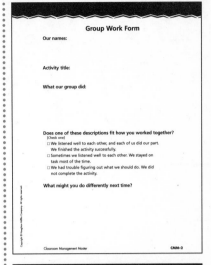

Reinforcing, discussing, monitoring, and praising group social skills will establish a foundation for effectively working with people in all types of groups and work contexts.

Combination Classrooms

Combination classrooms vary from district to district. Many combine two grade levels; some combine students based on abilities and needs; some include a wider range, across several levels. If you have a combination classroom, you know management poses unique challenges. You must ensure that all students have opportunities for direct instruction, have the appropriate reading materials, and have activities and resources needed to achieve expectations.

Students in combination classrooms interact and learn from students of different ages. "Self starters" and students who work well in independent groups may thrive in a combination environment. For all students, assessment is critical, so that they can be grouped flexibly and appropriately.

• **Reading texts** If you have only one grade level text for two levels of students, use the anthology as "community reading" material that all are exposed to, and then use the paperbacks for instruction, especially for on-level and above-level reading.

When both levels of text are available, conduct reading and instruction in flexible groups with the appropriate grade-level material. You may want to organize instruction and independent work using a chart, like the one shown here.

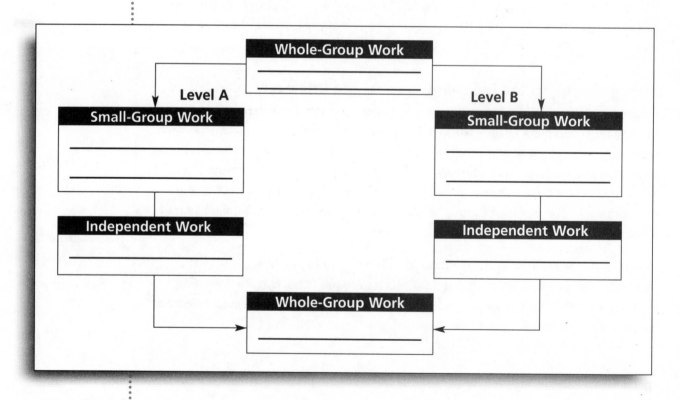

- **Record keeping** You may need to prepare tracking charts by grade level if you are responsible for meeting more than one level of expectations.

- **Who can help?** Recruit class parents, paraprofessionals, or members of the school-parent organization to help you facilitate the independent work of other students while you are providing direct instruction. One scenario might be that your aide supervises follow-up practice for Level A students while you introduce and teach a lesson to the Level B group. The next day, you and the aide "trade" levels. You introduce and teach Level A; the aiide supervises the lesson follow up with Level B.

Successful combination classroom management involves open and frequent communication with your principal or administrator, with peers, with parents or guardians, and with the students themselves. Continually monitor student progress and solicit feedback directly or through Group Work Forms to help you evaluate your flexible grouping plans.

TIME MANAGEMENT AND OTHER TIPS

The *Houghton Mifflin Reading* Teacher's Edition and the universal access handbooks give you comprehensive instruction, resources, and planning at your fingertips—saving you valuable time. What may steal time however, are the transitions, interruptions, and administrative responsibilities you face every day.

There are numerous strategies and short cuts teachers take and share with other teachers. List making, for example, is invaluable for ensuring that you don't miss important obligations. List everything you can, long term and short term, that you need to get done. Prioritize and reorder the items, and give yourself reasonable deadlines. After several list-making sessions over time, you'll get better at realizing what's possible to accomplish on a daily or weekly basis—and you'll have the satisfaction of crossing items off as you complete them.

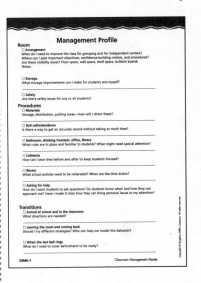

Another strategy for time management is to create a management picture for yourself. (See the Management Profile at the back of this handbook.) What is your day like? What eats up your time? What strategies can you use? The Management Profile checklist can help you anticipate many aspects of your day and plan in advance how you will deal with specific issues. As you work through the list, think of who can help with each item—students, families, colleagues, administrative personnel—and what things can be accomplished in stages rather than all at once.

Management Tips

The tips below cover a variety of management issues. Many may be familiar to you. Use them as quick reminders, or make notes next to them to include other related management strategies you use.

Keep a reminder list handy

Besides a daily "to-do" list, your reminders might include: Make sure everyone gets a chance to respond; Rephrase questions and affirm correct responses; Be patient; Reward creative thinking when it's appropriate, and so forth.

Encourage independence with handouts and posters

Prepare in advance materials to reinforce successful independent work, such as providing guidelines for reading with a partner or for reading a story aloud. See the "What I Can Do" chart (blackline master at the back of this handbook), for suggestions on how students can best use their "down time."

Write a contract for classroom discussions

For classroom discussions to be their most effective, set ground rules. Brainstorm rules and talk about what a successful discussion should include. Post the responses in a chart. Refer to the chart before discussions as a reminder to students.

Foster smooth transition times

Announce ahead of time that in three minutes, the current activity will end. Announce what the next activity will be. This gives students time to clean up or gather needed materials.

Distribute materials

Plan in stages. Distribute materials yourself before school, during recess, or after school. Note any issues that might arise for student monitors, whom you will train to help. Finally, once the process has been modeled and shared, shift the responsibility to students to collect and replace materials quietly.

Take notes for next time

Great ideas and useful self-evaluations can be easily forgotten in the intensity of each day. Use adhesive notes to attach your thoughts to pages so they're readily available for "next time."

Post a classroom behavior code

List and post behaviors that are expected, allowed, and not allowed in the classroom. Go over the list with students at the beginning of the year and frequently remind students of items on this list. Decide in advance how you will positively reinforce adherence to the code and how you will handle "violations."

Change the tempo

What should you do when you feel you've lost control and there's too much to do? Instead of hurrying forward, slow your pace. Spend a day working with students as slowly as necessary to get a renewed sense of control. You'll restore your leadership in their eyes.

Talk with every student, every day

Set a goal to touch base with each student every day. Keep a list in front of you and tally your contact with individuals or track their daily participation.

Regroup

Make sure each student is given an opportunity to participate in varied grouping situations. After the testing at the end of each theme, reevaluate and regroup students as needed.

For Further Reading:

Barr, R. (1995). What research says about grouping in the past and present and what it suggests about the future. In M. C. Randencich & L. J. McKay (Eds.), Flexible grouping for literacy in the elementary grades (pp. 1-24). Needham Heights: Allyn & Bacon.

Bear, D., Invernizzi, M., Templeton, S., & Johnston, F. (2000). Words their way: Word study for phonics, vocabulary, and spelling instruction (2nd ed.). Upper Saddle River, NJ: Merrill/Prentice-Hall.

Berghoff, B., & Egawa, K. (1998). No more "rocks": Grouping to give students control of their learning. In R. L. Allington (Ed.), Teaching struggling readers: Advice for helping children with reading/learning disabilities. Newark, DE: International Reading Association, pp. 61-67.

Cooper, J. D. (2000). Literacy: Helping children construct meaning. Boston, MA: Houghton Mifflin Company.

Good, T. L., & Brophy, J. E. (1997). Looking in classrooms (7th ed.). New York: Longman.

Johnson, D. W., & Johnson, R. T. (1972). Learning together and alone: Cooperation, competition, and individualization. Englewood Cliffs, NJ: Prentice-Hall.

Johnson, D. W., & Johnson, R. T. (1999). The three C's of school and classroom management. In J. Freiberg (Ed.), Beyond behaviorism (pp. 119-144). Boston: Allyn & Bacon.

Juel, C. (1990). The effects of reading group assignment on reading development in first and second grade. Journal of Reading Behavior, 22, 233-254.

Nagel, G. K (2001). Effective grouping for literacy instruction. Needham Heights, MA: Allyn & Bacon.

Oakes, J. (1985). Keeping track: How schools structure inequality. New Haven, CT: Yale University Press.

Palinscar, A. S., & Brown, A. L. (1984). Reciprocal teaching of comprehension-fostering and comprehension-monitoring activities. Cognition and Instruction, 1, 117-175.

Schell, L. M., & Rouch, R. L. (1988). The low reading group: An instructional and social dilemma. Journal of Reading Education, 14, 18-23.

Vogt, M. E. (1996). Creating a response-centered curriculum with literature discussion groups. In L. B. Gambrell, & J. F. Almasi (Eds.), Lively discussions! Fostering engaged reading. Newark, DE: International Reading Association.

Vogt, M. E. (2000). Content learning for students needing modifications: An issue of access. In M. McLaughlin & M. E. Vogt (Eds.). Creativity and innovation in content area teaching. Norwood, MA: Christopher-Gordon Publishing Company.

Walkthrough

To the Teacher

This walkthrough will familiarize you with the Assignment Planner that precedes the activities for each selection in this handbook. The Assignment Planner will help you and organize your materials for each selection as you use the three handbooks to provide universal access to various groups.

Before Assigning Activities

- Assemble materials needed for the activities on the following pages or in the *Challenge Handbook*. Pencils and writing paper are assumed.

- Students need to have read the literature appropriate to their ability level.

- Photocopy pages listed on this Assignment Planner

Additional Activities and Resources

This summarizes resources in the Additional Activities on the following pages and in the Challenge Handbook.

- These are in the *Practice Books* and the *Teacher's Editions* and accompanying *Teacher's Resource Blackline Masters*.

- Technology resources are for the major selection.

- Other resources are usually in the Houghton Mifflin classroom bookshelf collections.

Independent Activities

The left-hand page previews the assignments you will give to groups when they work independently.

These Masters and Teacher support pages are in the *Classroom Management Handbook.*

These Masters and Teacher support pages are in the *Challenge Handbook.*

ASSIGNMENT PLANNER

THEME 1/SELECTION 1: *Dragon Gets By*

Assignments for Independent Activities

Assign for On-Level Students

Masters: CM 1-1—CM 1-4
Teacher support: GO-1, GO-9
Classroom materials: Encyclopedia, dictionary, drawing paper, crayons, markers, index cards, almanacs, oaktag cards

Note: Many activities are appropriate for Extra Support students and English Language Learners.

Check that students have read the selection or leveled reading specified for an activity.

- Anthology, pp. 18–41: *Dragon Gets By;* "Roly-Poly"
- Phonics Library: *Len and Linda's Picnic; An Ice Cream Crash*

Assign for Challenge Students

Masters: CH 1-1, CH 1-2
Teacher support: GO-3
Classroom materials: See list of materials with each activity.

Note: Many activities are appropriate for advanced English Language Learners.

- Theme Paperbacks: *Fluff and the Long Nap* (On My Way Practice Reader); *The Adventures of Sugar and Junior* (On Level); *Rats on the Roof* (Challenge)
Provide copies of activity masters, graphic organizer masters, and challenge masters, as needed.

Additional Activities and Program Resources

Additional independent activities for this selection:

- Practice Book, pp. 3, 7, 11, 12, 13, 15, 16, 17, 231
- Teacher's Resources Blackline Masters, Theme 1 Reading Cards 2, 3
- TE pp. R5, R11, R17, R25, R28
- TE Challenge pp. 11, 34, 36, 41, 41H, R5, R11, R17, R25

Other program resources:

- Suggested in activities for this selection: Houghton Mifflin Science DiscoveryWorks Trade Books: *Emmett's Snowball*
- Students' self-selected independent reading materials
- Students' journals or other independent writing materials

Technology

Get Set to Read *Dragon Gets By*
Education Place: www.eduplace.com for more activities related to *Dragon Gets By*
Accelerated Reader® *Dragon Gets By*
Audiotape, *Dragon Gets By*

2 THEME 1: **Silly Stories**

- Always listed are independent reading and writing.

These lessons are in the *Extra Support Handbook.*

These lessons are in the *Handbook for English Language Learners.*

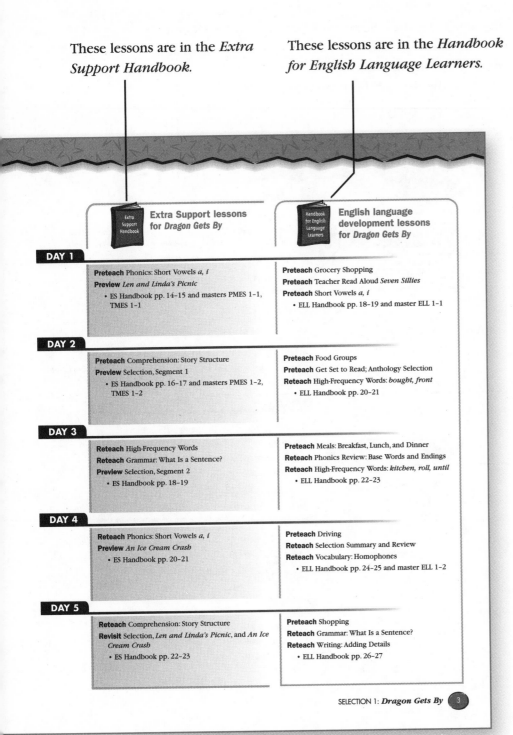

Extra Support lessons for *Dragon Gets By*

English language development lessons for *Dragon Gets By*

DAY 1

Preteach Phonics: Short Vowels *a, i*
Preview *Len and Linda's Picnic*
  • ES Handbook pp. 14–15 and masters PMES 1-1, TMES 1-1

Preteach Grocery Shopping
Preteach Teacher Read Aloud *Seven Sillies*
Preteach Short Vowels *a, i*
  • ELL Handbook pp. 18–19 and master ELL 1-1

DAY 2

Preteach Comprehension: Story Structure
Preview Selection, Segment 1
  • ES Handbook pp. 16–17 and masters PMES 1-2, TMES 1-2

Preteach Food Groups
Preteach Get Set to Read; Anthology Selection
Reteach High-Frequency Words: *bought, front*
  • ELL Handbook pp. 20–21

DAY 3

Reteach High-Frequency Words
Reteach Grammar: What Is a Sentence?
Preview Selection, Segment 2
  • ES Handbook pp. 18–19

Preteach Meals: Breakfast, Lunch, and Dinner
Reteach Phonics Review: Base Words and Endings
Reteach High-Frequency Words: *kitchen, roll, until*
  • ELL Handbook pp. 22–23

DAY 4

Reteach Phonics: Short Vowels *a, i*
Preview *An Ice Cream Crash*
  • ES Handbook pp. 20–21

Preteach Driving
Reteach Selection Summary and Review
Reteach Vocabulary: Homophones
  • ELL Handbook pp. 24–25 and master ELL 1-2

DAY 5

Reteach Comprehension: Story Structure
Revisit Selection, *Len and Linda's Picnic*, and *An Ice Cream Crash*
  • ES Handbook pp. 22–23

Preteach Shopping
Reteach Grammar: What Is a Sentence?
Reteach Writing: Adding Details
  • ELL Handbook pp. 26–27

SELECTION 1: *Dragon Gets By* 3

Extra Support and English Language Development

The right-hand page previews the lessons you will teach other groups, using the *Extra Support Handbook* and the *Handbook for English Language Learners.*

In the *Extra Support Handbook,* lessons are presented in a five-day plan that includes

• preteaching to prepare students for whole-class instruction

• reteaching after core instruction to provide more practice

• a literature focus in the form of guided previews or revisiting selections or ancillary literature

In the *Handbook for English Language Learners,* lessons are presented in a five-day plan that includes

• language development that introduces background and vocabulary and supports students' acquisition of English vocabulary

• literature focus that provides opportunities for students to preview and review the selection

• skill focus that provides preview and/ or review of selected skills

Walkthrough of Activities

This part of the walkthrough will familiarize you with the five-day plan that is provided for independent activities for each selection in this level of *Houghton Mifflin Reading: A Legacy of Literacy*. Annotations in this walkthrough indicate the major features on these pages.

Additional Activities

Additional Activities are independent work that can be found elsewhere in materials for Houghton Mifflin Reading, referenced here on the appropriate day as a reminder to use them.

Content Area

Any content-area connection is given at the end of the notes for the teacher.

English Language Learners

Adaptations are provided when activities can be made more accessible to English Language Learners.

Materials

Materials needed, other than paper and pencil, are listed. Some activities need Graphic Organizer Masters, which are in the Blackline Masters section at the back of this handbook.

Time; Grouping

- Approximate amount of time an activity takes
- Recommendation for grouping—individual, pair, or small group.

Activities

SELECTION 1:
Dragon Gets By

Activity Master CM 1–1

THEME 1: *Dragon Gets By*

Name _____

1. Imaginary Creatures
Compare and contrast Dragon with another imaginary creature that you have read about. Make two lists. Label the first list *Same*, the second *Different*. When writing words in your lists, think about
- how the creatures look and act
- where the creatures live
- what the creatures eat
Share your lists with the class.

2. Dragon's Lair
The dragon in *Dragon Gets By* lived in a house. But in most stories, dragons live in a cave called a *lair*. Make a list of animals. Then next to each animal write the name of the place where they live. If you need to, look up the animals' homes in an encyclopedia. When you finish your list, choose one animal and draw a picture of it living in its home. Under the picture, write a sentence that describes the animal and its home.

3. Silly Snack
Make up a recipe for a silly snack. Use your favorite foods as ingredients. For example: peanut butter, apples, and raisins on a cracker. Write your recipe on an index card. Show it to a classmate. Would he or she eat the snack? Why or why not?

CM 1–1 Activity Master   Grade 2 • Theme 1: Silly Stories

Activity Master CM 1–2

THEME 1: *Dragon Gets By*

Name _____

4. Dragon Noises
Imagine the different sounds a dragon might make. Do its wings beat when it flies? Does it breathe fire? Working with a partner, create a list of six sound words that describe the sounds a dragon might make. Together, write sentences using the words in your list.

5. Make a Match!
Play this matching game with a classmate.
- Make a list of the vocabulary words and their meanings from *Dragon Gets By*. The words are on page 5 of the Practice Book. You will use this list as your answer key.
- Write each vocabulary word on an index card. Write each meaning on a different index card.
- Arrange the word cards face up on your desk. Place the meaning cards in a pile face down.
- Have a classmate choose a meaning card from the top of the pile and try to match it with a word. If the match is correct, he or she keeps the cards. If the match is incorrect, he or she places the meaning card on the bottom of the pile. Keep playing until all the meanings have been matched.

Grade 2 • Theme 1: Silly Stories   Activity Master CM 1–2

DAY 1

1. Imaginary Creatures <u>30 MIN.</u> INDIVIDUAL
Review the process of comparing and contrasting. Tell children that fairy tales, folktales, and movies are good sources for imaginary creatures.

English Language Learners Brainstorm a list of creatures with children.

2. Dragon's Lair <u>30 MIN.</u> INDIVIDUAL
Materials: encyclopedia, dictionary, drawing paper, crayons, and markers

Tell children to check the spelling of their words in a dictionary. Hang children's drawings on a class bulletin board. (Science)

Additional Activities
- Audio Tape, *Dragon Gets By*
- Practice Book, p. 3, Phonics
- Practice Book, p. 231, Spelling
- Technology: See p. 2.

DAY 2

3. Silly Snack <u>20 MIN.</u> INDIVIDUAL / PAIR
Materials: index card and sample recipe card

Show a sample recipe card to children as an example.

English Language Learners Review the word *ingredients*.

4. Dragon Noises <u>30 MIN.</u> INDIVIDUAL / PAIR
Explain to children that the sound of the words should resemble the sound made by the dragon. Give examples such as buzz (bee).

Additional Activities
- Practice Book, p. 7, Comprehension
- Practice Book, p. 11, Spelling
- Practice Book, p. 15, Grammar
- Technology: See p. 2.

DAY 3

5. Make a Match! <u>30 MIN.</u> INDIVIDUAL / PAIR
Materials: index cards

Have children write a silly sentence using each word.

 THEME 1: **Silly Stories**

The Activities on Masters

The ten numbered activities on these pages appear on four blackline masters to be used during the week.

6. The Dragon's World 30 MIN. INDIVIDUAL

Materials: crayons and markers

You might collect all the stories to create a class story book.

English Language Learners Explain to children how to write from their point of view, using first-person pronouns.

Additional Activities
• Practice Book, p. 12, Spelling
• Technology: See p. 2.

DAY 4

7. Group Story 20 MIN. SMALL GROUP

Review story structure with children. Tell children to be sure that each sentence they add builds upon the previous sentence.

8. Food Phrases 30 MIN. PAIR

Materials: index cards

Have children play this rhyming game with other words.

English Language Learners You might want to review rhyming.

Additional Activities
• Practice Book, p. 13, Spelling
• Practice Book, p. 16, Grammar
• Technology: See p. 2.

DAY 5

9. Grocery Riddles 40 MIN. INDIVIDUAL / PAIR

You may want to create a class riddle book out of the student riddles.

10. Follow That Dragon! 40 MIN. INDIVIDUAL / PAIR

Materials: crayons and drawing paper

Have children think how one story event leads to the next. Tell children to make their sentences describe what happens in their pictures.

English Language Learners Remind children about the meanings of the words *beginning, middle,* and *end.*

Additional Activities
• Anthology, pp. 36-37, Responding
• Practice Book, p. 17, Grammar
• TE p. R5, R11, R17, R25, R28
• Technology: See p. 2.

Activity Master CM 1–3

THEME 1/*Dragon Gets By*

Name _____

6. The Dragon's World
Imagine what life would be like if dragons were real and living near you, as in *Dragon Gets By.* Write a short story about meeting a dragon. Be sure to include
• a beginning, middle, and end to your story
• pictures for your story

7. Group Story
Create a group story about a dragon.
• One person in the group begins the story by saying a sentence.
• Each member of the group adds one sentence to the story, building on what has been said so far.
• The last sentence should be an ending to the story.

8. Food Phrases
Here's a game Dragon would love! It's all about food.
• Write ten food words on an index card.
• Exchange cards with a classmate.
• Make up a rhyme for each word on the card. Use a short phrase for each rhyme. For example, *dip the chip.* Write your rhyme on a separate sheet of paper.
• Share your rhymes with your classmate.

CM 1–3 Activity Master   Grade 2   Theme 1: Silly Stories

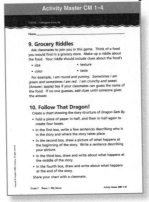

Activity Master CM 1–4

THEME 1/*Dragon Gets By*

Name _____

9. Grocery Riddles
Ask classmates to join you in this game. Think of a food you would find in a grocery store. Make up a riddle about the food. Your riddle should include clues about the food's
• size   • texture
• color   • taste
For example, *I am round and yummy. Sometimes I am green and sometimes I am red. I am crunchy and sweet.* (Answer: apple) See if your classmates can guess the name of the food. If no one guesses, add clues until someone gives the answer.

10. Follow That Dragon!
Create a chart showing the story structure of *Dragon Gets By.*
• Fold a piece of paper in half, and then in half again to create four boxes.
• In the first box, write a few sentences describing who is in the story and where the story takes place.
• In the second box, draw a picture of what happens at the beginning of the story. Write a sentence describing your picture.
• In the third box, draw and write about what happens at the middle of the story.
• In the fourth box, draw and write about what happens at the end of the story.
Share your chart with a classmate.

Grade 2   Theme 1: Silly Stories   Activity Master CM 1–4

Brief Notes About the Activity

Notes may suggest brief preparation assistance that children might need, or ways to share their completed work.

To Meet Individual Needs

Some activities are identified as being related to the easier leveled reading, such as Phonics Library or On My Way Practice Readers, and are particularly appropriate for children who need extra support.

Facsimile of Activity Master

Heading identifies the child's blackline master. A reduced facsimile is provided here. Full-size activity masters are in the Blackline Masters section of this handbook.

SELECTION 1: *Dragon Gets By* 5

ASSIGNMENT PLANNER

THEME 1/SELECTION 1: *Dragon Gets By*

Assignments for Independent Activities

Assign for On-Level Students

Masters: CM 1-1—CM 1-4

Teacher support: GO-1, GO-9

Classroom materials: Encyclopedia, dictionary, drawing paper, crayons, markers, index cards, almanacs, oaktag cards

Note: Many activities are appropriate for Extra Support students and English Language Learners.

Check that students have read the selection or leveled reading specified for an activity.

- Anthology, pp. 18–41: *Dragon Gets By;* "Roly-Poly"

- Phonics Library: *Len and Linda's Picnic; An Ice Cream Crash*

Assign for Challenge Students

Masters: CH 1-1, CH 1-2

Teacher support: GO-3

Classroom materials: See list of materials with each activity.

Note: Many activities are appropriate for advanced English Language Learners.

- Theme Paperbacks: *Fluff and the Long Nap* (On My Way Practice Reader); *The Adventures of Sugar and Junior* (On Level); *Rats on the Roof* (Challenge)

Provide copies of activity masters, graphic organizer masters, and challenge masters, as needed.

Additional Activities and Program Resources

Additional independent activities for this selection:

- Practice Book, pp. 3, 7, 11, 12, 13, 15, 16, 17, 231

- Teacher's Resources Blackline Masters, Theme 1 Reading Cards 2, 3

- TE pp. R5, R11, R17, R25, R28

- TE Challenge pp. 11, 34, 36, 41, 41H, R5, R11, R17, R25

Other program resources:

- Suggested in activities for this selection: Houghton Mifflin Science DiscoveryWorks Trade Books: *Emmett's Snowball*

- Students' self-selected independent reading materials

- Students' journals or other independent writing materials

Technology

Get Set to Read *Dragon Gets By*

Education Place: www.eduplace.com for more activities related to *Dragon Gets By*

Accelerated Reader®, *Dragon Gets By*

Audiotape, *Dragon Gets By*

Extra Support lessons for *Dragon Gets By*

English language development lessons for *Dragon Gets By*

DAY 1

Preteach Phonics: Short Vowels *a, i*
Preview *Len and Linda's Picnic*
- ES Handbook pp. 14–15 and masters PMES 1-1, TMES 1-1

Preteach Grocery Shopping
Preteach Teacher Read Aloud *Seven Sillies*
Preteach Short Vowels *a, i*
- ELL Handbook pp. 18–19 and master ELL 1-1

DAY 2

Preteach Comprehension: Story Structure
Preview Selection, Segment 1
- ES Handbook pp. 16–17 and masters PMES 1-2, TMES 1-2

Preteach Food Groups
Preteach Get Set to Read; Anthology Selection
Reteach High-Frequency Words: *bought, front*
- ELL Handbook pp. 20–21

DAY 3

Reteach High-Frequency Words
Reteach Grammar: What Is a Sentence?
Preview Selection, Segment 2
- ES Handbook pp. 18–19

Preteach Meals: Breakfast, Lunch, and Dinner
Reteach Phonics Review: Base Words and Endings
Reteach High-Frequency Words: *kitchen, roll, until*
- ELL Handbook pp. 22–23

DAY 4

Reteach Phonics: Short Vowels *a, i*
Preview *An Ice Cream Crash*
- ES Handbook pp. 20–21

Preteach Driving
Reteach Selection Summary and Review
Reteach Vocabulary: Homophones
- ELL Handbook pp. 24–25 and master ELL 1-2

DAY 5

Reteach Comprehension: Story Structure
Revisit Selection, *Len and Linda's Picnic*, and *An Ice Cream Crash*
- ES Handbook pp. 22–23

Preteach Shopping
Reteach Grammar: What Is a Sentence?
Reteach Writing: Adding Details
- ELL Handbook pp. 26–27

DAY 1

1. Imaginary Creatures 30 MIN. INDIVIDUAL

Review the process of comparing and contrasting. Tell children that fairy tales, folktales, and movies are good sources for imaginary creatures.

English Language Learners Brainstorm a list of creatures with children.

2. Dragon's Lair 30 MIN. INDIVIDUAL

Materials: encyclopedia, dictionary, drawing paper, crayons, and markers

Tell children to check the spelling of their words in a dictionary. Hang children's drawings on a class bulletin board. (Science)

Additional Activities

- Audio Tape, *Dragon Gets By*
- Practice Book, p. 3, Phonics
- Practice Book, p. 231, Spelling
- Technology: See p. 2.

DAY 2

3. Silly Snack 20 MIN. INDIVIDUAL / PAIR

Materials: index card and sample recipe card

Show a sample recipe card to children as an example.

English Language Learners Review the word *ingredients*.

4. Dragon Noises 30 MIN. INDIVIDUAL / PAIR

Explain to children that the sound of the words should resemble the sound made by the dragon. Give examples such as buzz (bee).

Additional Activities

- Practice Book, p. 7, Comprehension
- Practice Book, p. 11, Spelling
- Practice Book, p. 15, Grammar
- Technology: See p. 2.

DAY 3

5. Make a Match! 30 MIN. INDIVIDUAL / PAIR

Materials: index cards

Have children write a silly sentence using each word.

Activity Master CM 1–1

THEME 1/*Dragon Gets By*

Name _____

1. Imaginary Creatures
Compare and contrast Dragon with another imaginary creature that you have read about. Make two lists. Label the first list *Same*, the second *Different*. When writing words in your lists, think about
- how the creatures look and act
- where the creatures live
- what the creatures eat
Share your lists with the class.

2. Dragon's Lair
The dragon in *Dragon Gets By* lived in a house. But in most stories, dragons live in a cave called a *lair*. Make a list of animals. Then next to each animal write the name of the place where they live. If you need to, look up the animals' homes in an encyclopedia. When you finish your list, choose one animal and draw a picture of it living in its home. Under the picture, write a sentence that describes the animal and its home.

3. Silly Snack
Make up a recipe for a silly snack. Use your favorite foods as ingredients. For example: *peanut butter, apples,* and *raisins on a cracker.* Write your recipe on an index card. Show it to a classmate. Would he or she eat the snack? Why or why not?

CM 1–1 Activity Master   Grade 2   Theme 1: Silly Stories

Activity Master CM 1–2

THEME 1/*Dragon Gets By*

Name _____

4. Dragon Noises
Imagine the different sounds a dragon might make. Do its wings beat when it flies? Does it breathe fire? Working with a partner, create a list of six sound words that describe the sounds a dragon might make. Together, write sentences using the words in your list.

5. Make a Match!
Play this matching game with a classmate.
- Make a list of the vocabulary words and their meanings from *Dragon Gets By.* The words are on page 5 of the Practice Book. You will use this list as your answer key.
- Write each vocabulary word on an index card. Write each meaning on a different index card.
- Arrange the word cards face up on your desk. Place the meaning cards in a pile face down.
- Have a classmate choose a meaning card from the top of the pile and try to match it with a word. If the match is correct, he or she keeps the cards. If the match is incorrect, he or she places the meaning card on the bottom of the pile. Keep playing until all the meanings have been matched.

Grade 2   Theme 1: Silly Stories   Activity Master CM 1–2

6. The Dragon's World 30 MIN. INDIVIDUAL

Materials: *crayons and markers*

You might collect all the stories to create a class story book.

English Language Learners Explain to children how to write from their point of view, using first-person pronouns.

Additional Activities
- Practice Book, p. 12, Spelling
- Technology: See p. 2.

DAY 4

7. Group Story 20 MIN. SMALL GROUP

Review story structure with children. Tell children to be sure that each sentence they add builds upon the previous sentence.

8. Food Phrases 30 MIN. PAIR

Materials: *index cards*

Have children play this rhyming game with other words.

English Language Learners You might want to review rhyming.

Additional Activities
- Practice Book, p. 13, Spelling
- Practice Book, p. 16, Grammar
- Technology: See p. 2.

DAY 5

9. Grocery Riddles 40 MIN. INDIVIDUAL / PAIR

You may want to create a class riddle book out of the student riddles.

10. Follow That Dragon! 40 MIN. INDIVIDUAL / PAIR

Materials: *crayons and drawing paper*

Have children think how one story event leads to the next. Tell children to make their sentences describe what happens in their pictures.

English Language Learners Remind children about the meanings of the words *beginning, middle,* and *end.*

Additional Activities
- Anthology, pp. 36-37, Responding
- Practice Book, p. 17, Grammar
- TE p. R5, R11, R17, R25, R28
- Technology: See p. 2.

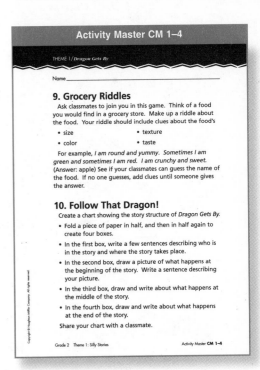

Activity Master CM 1–3

THEME 1/*Dragon Gets By*

Name_____

6. The Dragon's World
Imagine what life would be like if dragons were real and living near you, as in *Dragon Gets By.* Write a short story about meeting a dragon. Be sure to include
- a beginning, middle, and end to your story
- pictures for your story

7. Group Story
Create a group story about a dragon.
- One person in the group begins the story by saying a sentence.
- Each member of the group adds one sentence to the story, building on what has been said so far.
- The last sentence should be an ending to the story.

8. Food Phrases
Here's a game Dragon would love! It's all about food.
- Write ten food words on an index card.
- Exchange cards with a classmate.
- Make up a rhyme for each word on the card. Use a short phrase for each rhyme. For example, *dip the chip.* Write your rhyme on a separate sheet of paper.
- Share your rhymes with your classmate.

CM 1–3 Activity Master   Grade 2   Theme 1: Silly Stories

Activity Master CM 1–4

THEME 1/*Dragon Gets By*

Name_____

9. Grocery Riddles
Ask classmates to join you in this game. Think of a food you would find in a grocery store. Make up a riddle about the food. Your riddle should include clues about the food's
- size
- color
- texture
- taste

For example, *I am round and yummy. Sometimes I am green and sometimes I am red. I am crunchy and sweet.* (Answer: apple) See if your classmates can guess the name of the food. If no one guesses, add clues until someone gives the answer.

10. Follow That Dragon!
Create a chart showing the story structure of *Dragon Gets By.*
- Fold a piece of paper in half, and then in half again to create four boxes.
- In the first box, write a few sentences describing who is in the story and where the story takes place.
- In the second box, draw a picture of what happens at the beginning of the story. Write a sentence describing your picture.
- In the third box, draw and write about what happens at the middle of the story.
- In the fourth box, draw and write about what happens at the end of the story.
Share your chart with a classmate.

Grade 2   Theme 1: Silly Stories   Activity Master **CM 1–4**

THEME 1/SELECTION 2: *Julius*

Assignments for Independent Activities

Assign for On-Level Students

Masters: CM 1–5—CM 1–8

Teacher support: GO-1, GO-9

Classroom materials: Encyclopedia, drawing paper, crayons, markers, dictionary, index cards, silly stories from the classroom library

Note: Many activities are appropriate for Extra Support students and English Language Learners.

Assign for Challenge Students

Masters: CH 1–3, CH 1–4

Teacher support: GO-3

Classroom materials: Crayons, markers, drawing paper, poster board, other art supplies as needed

Note: Many activities are appropriate for advanced English Language Learners.

Check that students have read the selection or leveled reading specified for an activity.

- Anthology, pp. 46–79: *Julius;* "It's Easy to Be Polite"
- Phonics Library: *Big Hog's House Hunt; Robin's Farm*

- Theme Paperbacks: *Fluff and the Long Nap* (On My Way Practice Reader); *The Adventures of Sugar and Junior* (On Level); *Rats on the Roof* (Challenge)

Provide copies of activity masters, graphic organizer masters, and challenge masters, as needed.

Additional Activities and Program Resources

Additional independent activities for this selection:

- Practice Book, pp. 25, 29, 32, 33, 34, 35, 37, 38, 39, 233
- Teacher's Resources Blackline Masters, Theme 1 Reading Cards 5, 6, 7
- TE pp. R7, R13, R19, R26, R28
- TE Challenge pp. 72, 79, 79H, 80G, R7, R13, R19, R26

Other program resources:

- Suggested in activities for this selection: Houghton Mifflin Science DiscoveryWorks Trade Books: *Emmett's Snowball*
- Students' self-selected independent reading materials
- Students' journals or other independent writing materials

Technology

Get Set to Read *Julius*

Education Place: www.eduplace.com for more activities related to *Julius*

Accelerated Reader®, *Julius*

Audiotape, *Julius*

Extra Support lessons for *Julius*

English language development lessons for *Julius*

DAY 1

Preteach Phonics: Short Vowels *o, u, e*
Preteach Structural Analysis: VCCV Pattern
Preview *Big Hog's House Hunt*
  • ES Handbook pp. 24–25 and masters PMES 1–3, TMES 1–3

Preteach Invitations
Preteach Teacher Read Aloud *Daddy, Could I Have an Elephant?*
Preteach Phonics: Short Vowels *o, u, e;* VCCV Pattern
  • ELL Handbook pp. 28–29 and master ELL 1–4

DAY 2

Preteach Comprehension: Fantasy and Realism
Preview Selection, Segment 1
  • ES Handbook pp. 26–27 and masters PMES 1–4, TMES 1–4

Preteach Seasons
Preteach Get Set to Read; Anthology Selection
Reteach High-Frequency Words: *brought, reason*
  • ELL Handbook pp. 30–31

DAY 3

Reteach High-Frequency Words
Reteach Grammar: Naming Parts of Sentences
Preview Selection, Segment 2
  • ES Handbook pp. 28–29

Preteach Things We Wear
Reteach Phonics Review: Short Vowels *a, i*
Reteach High-Frequency Words: *special, surprise*
  • ELL Handbook pp. 32–33

DAY 4

Reteach Phonics: Short Vowels *o, u, e*
Reteach Structure Analysis: VCCV Pattern
Preview *Robin's Farm*
  • ES Handbook pp. 30–31

Preteach States
Reteach Selection Summary and Review
Reteach Vocabulary: Synonyms
  • ELL Handbook pp. 34–35 and master ELL 1–5

DAY 5

Reteach Comprehension: Fantasy and Realism
Revisit Selection, *Big Hog's House Hunt*, and *Robin's Farm*
  • ES Handbook pp. 32–33

Preteach Manners
Reteach Grammar: Naming Parts of Sentences
Reteach Writing: Writing Dates
  • ELL Handbook pp. 36–37

Activities

Activity Master CM 1–5

Name_____

1. Alaskan Animals

In the story *Julius*, Maya receives an Alaskan pig from her grandfather. What other kinds of animals live in Alaska?

- Look up Alaska in an encyclopedia or other reference source. Make a list of all the animals that live there. Note any important details you find about them.
- Choose one of those animals and draw a picture of it. Under your picture, write three or four sentences that talk about what Alaskan animal you chose and why.

Share your drawings with the class.

2. Pet Names

Julius is the name Maya gave her pet pig. What name would you give an unusual pet?

- Make a list of five unusual pets. For example: *elephant, monkey,* or *boa constrictor.*
- What if these animals were your pets? What names would you give them? Write your choices next to each animal. Choose your favorite unusual pet.

Write a letter to a friend telling him or her about your favorite new pet. In your letter, talk about

- where you keep it
- what you feed it
- what problems you have with it
- how you solve the problems

Activity Master CM 1–6

Name_____

3. Pig Riddles

Use the code to answer the following riddle:

A	B	C	D	E	F	G	H	I	J	K	L	M	N	O	P	Q	R	S	T	U	V	W	X	Y	Z
1	2	3	4	5	6	7	8	9	10	11	12	13	14	15	16	17	18	19	20	21	22	23	24	25	26

What kind of bath do pigs like?

8   15   7   23   1   19   8

_____

Make a pig riddle of your own. Write the question on an index card. Draw a line for each letter of the answer. Write the code for the missing letters over the lines. Give your riddle to a classmate or family member to solve. If you need help, look up words in the dictionary that begin with *pig* or *hog*.

4. *Fluff and the Long Nap/The Adventures of Sugar and Junior*

Think about the main characters in either *Fluff and the Long Nap* or *The Adventures of Sugar and Junior.* What other adventures might they have? Write a new adventure for one of the stories. Before you write, first review the story and answer these questions:

- What will the setting be?
- What will happen in the new chapter? What is its plot?
- Will the new chapter be funny or serious? Will it include fantasy or realism?

Write your adventure. Trade stories with a classmate. Talk about what you liked about each other's work.

DAY 1

1. Alaskan Animals <u>30 MIN.</u> INDIVIDUAL

Materials: encyclopedia, drawing paper, crayons, and markers

Display drawings on a bulletin board. (Social Studies) (Science)

2. Pet Names <u>30 MIN.</u> INDIVIDUAL

Materials: dictionary

Tell children to check the spelling of their words in a dictionary. (Science)

English Language Learners Encourage children from different countries to include animals that might be native to their place of birth.

> ### Additional Activities
>
> - Audio Tape, *Julius*
> - Practice Book, p. 25, Phonics
> - Practice Book, p. 233, Spelling
> - Technology: See p. 6.

DAY 2

3. Pig Riddles <u>30 MIN.</u> INDIVIDUAL / PAIR

Materials: index cards and dictionary

Children should get the answer: HOGWASH. If necessary, explain how the code works. You might want to create a class riddle as an example.

4. *Fluff and the Long Nap* (On My Way Practice Reader)/*The Adventures of Sugar and Junior* (On-Level Theme paperback) <u>60 MIN.</u> INDIVIDUAL

Remind students to reread the story carefully.

> ### Additional Activities
>
> - Practice Book, p. 29, Comprehension
> - Practice Book, p. 33, Spelling
> - Practice Book, p. 37, Grammar
> - Technology: See p. 6.

DAY 3

5. Fact or Fiction <u>30 MIN.</u> INDIVIDUAL / PAIR

Materials: Graphic Organizer Master 9

Give examples by making a few of the fantastic elements realistic. Ask volunteers to read their new versions of the story to the class.

6. Silly Rhymes   30 MIN.   INDIVIDUAL / PAIR
Materials: *Graphic Organizer Master 1*

Ask volunteers to read their rhymes to the class.

English Language Learners Review with children what a rhyme is.

> ### Additional Activities
> • Practice Book, p. 34, Spelling   • Technology: See p. 6.

DAY 4

7. Miss Manners   30 MIN.   INDIVIDUAL
Materials: *drawing paper*

Talk with children about why manners are important.

8. Tricky Pictures   30 MIN.   INDIVIDUAL / PAIR
Materials: *silly stories from the classroom library*

Explain to children that artists add details to a picture to make it more interesting or funny and to give the reader a visual image to go with their story.

> ### Additional Activities
> • Practice Book, p. 32, Phonics   • Practice Book, p. 38, Grammar
> • Practice Book, p. 35, Spelling   • Technology: See p. 6.

DAY 5

9. Fill It In!   30 MIN.   INDIVIDUAL / PAIR
Materials: *index cards*

If children have trouble creating sentences, tell them to reread how the word is used in the story.

English Language Learners Pair children with fluent English speakers.

10. Postcard From Grandfather
Materials: *encyclopedia, almanacs, oaktag cards, and crayons*

Remind children that a postcard usually has a picture on one side and a message on the other. (Social Studies)

> ### Additional Activities
> • Anthology, pp. 74–75, Responding   • TE p. R7, R13, R19, R26, R28
> • Practice Book, p. 39, Grammar   • Technology: See p. 6.

THEME 1/SELECTION 3: *Mrs. Brown Went to Town*

Assignments for Independent Activities

Assign for On-Level Students

Classroom Management Handbook

Masters: CM 1-9—CM 1-12
Teacher support: GO-1, GO-9
Classroom materials: See list of materials with each activity.

Note: Many activities are appropriate for Extra Support students and English Language Learners.

Assign for Challenge Students

Challenge Handbook

Masters: CH 1-5, CH 1-6
Teacher support: GO-3
Classroom materials: See list of materials with each activity.

Note: Many activities are appropriate for advanced English Language Learners.

Check that students have read the selection or leveled reading specified for an activity.

- Anthology, pp. 82–111: *Mrs. Brown Went to Town;* "Oodles of Riddles"
- Phonics Library: *Jane's Mistake; The Big Surprise*

- Theme Paperbacks: *Fluff and the Long Nap* (On My Way Practice Reader); *The Adventures of Sugar and Junior* (On Level); *Rats on the Roof* (Challenge)

Provide copies of activity masters, graphic organizer masters, and challenge masters, as needed.

Additional Activities and Program Resources

Additional independent activities for this selection:

- Practice Book, pp. 42, 46, 50, 51, 52, 54, 55, 56, 233
- Teacher's Resources Blackline Masters, Theme 1 Reading Cards 9, 10, 11
- TE pp. R9, R15, R21, R27, R29
- TE Challenge pp. 106, 111, 111H, 113, R9, R15, R21, R25, R29

Other program resources:

- Suggested in activities for this selection: Houghton Mifflin Science DiscoveryWorks Trade Books: *Emmett's Snowball*
- Students' self-selected independent reading materials
- Students' journals or other independent writing materials

Technology

Get Set to Read *Mrs. Brown Went to Town*

Education Place: www.eduplace.com for more activities related to *Mrs. Brown Went to Town*

Accelerated Reader®, *Mrs. Brown Went to Town*

Audiotape, *Mrs. Brown Went to Town*

Extra Support lessons for *Mrs. Brown Went to Town*

English language development lessons for *Mrs. Brown Went to Town*

DAY 1

Preteach Phonics: Long Vowels CVCe: *a, i*
Preview *Jane's Mistake*
- ES Handbook pp. 34–35 and masters PMES 1–5, TMES 1–5

Preteach Farm Animals
Preteach Teacher Read Aloud *Lemonade Stand*
Preteach Phonics: Long Vowels CVCe: *a, i*
- ELL Handbook pp. 38–39 and master ELL 1–7

DAY 2

Preteach Comprehension: Predicting Outcomes
Preview Selection, Segment 1
- ES Handbook pp. 36–37 and masters PMES 1–6, TMES 1–6

Preteach Hospitals
Preteach Get Set to Read; Anthology Selection
Reteach High-Frequency Words: *different, letter, word*
- ELL Handbook pp. 40–41

DAY 3

Reteach High Frequency Words
Reteach Grammar: Action Parts of a Sentence
Preview Selection, Segment 2
- ES Handbook pp. 38–39

Preteach Rooms of a House
Reteach Phonics Review: Short Vowels *o, u, e*
Reteach High-Frequency Words: *floor, move, poor*
- ELL Handbook pp. 42–43

DAY 4

Reteach Phonics: Long Vowels CVCe: *a, i*
Preview *The Big Surprise*
- ES Handbook pp. 40–41

Preteach Colors
Reteach Selection Summary and Review
Reteach Vocabulary: Multiple-Meaning Words
- ELL Handbook pp. 44–45 and master ELL 1–8

DAY 5

Reteach Comprehension: Predicting Outcomes
Revisit *Jane's Mistake*, Selection, and *The Big Surprise*
- ES Handbook pp. 42–43

Preteach Vehicles
Reteach Grammar: Action Parts of Sentences
Reteach Writing: Voice
- ELL Handbook pp. 46–47

DAY 1

1. Silly Sentences 30 MIN. INDIVIDUAL / PAIR
If necessary, review complete sentences with children.

English Language Learners Invite students to explain what makes the sentences silly.

2. Many Meanings 30 MIN. PAIR
Explain how a word can have two meanings. Brainstorm examples with children.

Additional Activities

• Audio Tape, *Mrs. Brown Went to Town*
• Practice Book, p. 42, Phonics
• Practice Book, p. 233, Spelling
• Technology: See p. 10.

DAY 2

3. Barnyard Poster 30 MIN. INDIVIDUAL
Materials: scissors, posterboard, and old magazines

When the children are finished, display their posters on a classroom bulletin board. (Art)

4. Caught in the Act! 30 MIN. INDIVIDUAL
Materials: drawing paper

Brainstorm with students some of the reactions Mrs. Brown might have. Talk with children about what the animals are doing that they should not.

Additional Activities

• Practice Book, p. 46, Comprehension
• Practice Book, p. 50, Spelling
• Practice Book, p. 54, Grammar
• Technology: See p. 10.

DAY 3

5. Take a Vote 30 MIN. INDIVIDUAL
Materials: drawing paper

Explain the word *vote* to children. Use elections as an example of how voting works. Explain how voting is a way to choose people to run our government. (Social studies) (Math)

6. Rhyming Circle   20 MIN.   SMALL GROUP

Explain how a continuous rhyming activity works. Review with children what rhymes are. Remind them that all the words they rhyme must be real words, not nonsense words.

Additional Activities

- Practice Book, p. 51, Spelling
- Technology: See p. 10.

DAY 4

7. Word Jumble   30 MIN.   INDIVIDUAL / PAIR

Materials: 37 2-inch by 2-inch squares of paper for each child playing

You might want to pick a word and demonstrate the lettering and numbering system to the class.

8. Farm Life   40 MIN.   INDIVIDUAL

Materials: drawing paper, encyclopedia

Ask volunteers to share their paragraphs with the class

Additional Activities

- Practice Book, p. 52, Spelling
- Practice Book, p. 55, Grammar
- Technology: See p. 10.

DAY 5

9. Story to Song!   30 MIN.   SMALL GROUP

Remind children that their songs should reflect what happens in the selection. Allow time for children to practice their songs and perform them for the class. (Music)

10. Weather Reporter   30 MIN.   INDIVIDUAL

Tell children that meteorologists predict the weather before it happens. Talk about where students can find a weather report. Make a list of the symbols meteorologists use to illustrate the weather (Science)

Additional Activities

- Anthology, pp. 74–75, Responding
- Practice Book, p. 56, Grammar
- TE p. R9, R15, R21, R27, R29
- Technology: See p. 10.

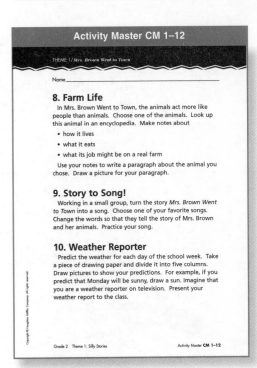

Activity Master CM 1–11

THEME 1/*Mrs. Brown Went to Town*

Name _____

6. Rhyming Circle
Did you notice the rhymes in *Mrs. Brown Went to Town*? Sit in a circle and share a rhyme.

- The first person says a word. The person to his or her right says a word that rhymes with the first word. The next person says another word that rhymes.
- Continue until all players have said a rhyming word.
- Then the next person begins with a new word. Everyone takes turns saying rhyming words again.
- Continue the rhyming circle until all the members have introduced a new word.

7. Word Jumble
Follow these directions to play a jumble word game.

- Make a numbered list of all the vocabulary words on page 44 of the Practice Book.
- On the 2-inch squares of paper, write each letter from the first word on your list.
- On the backs of each of the letters of the word, write the number of the word. This is in case you forget which letters go with which words.
- Continue steps two and three until you have made letter squares for all the words.
- Mix up each of the word's letters. Lay the letters on your desk.
- Ask a classmate to put the letters in the correct order and use the word in a sentence.

CM 1–11 Activity Master   Grade 2 Theme 1: Silly Stories

Activity Master CM 1–12

THEME 1/*Mrs. Brown Went to Town*

Name _____

8. Farm Life
In Mrs. Brown Went to Town, the animals act more like people than animals. Choose one of the animals. Look up this animal in an encyclopedia. Make notes about

- how it lives
- what it eats
- what its job might be on a real farm

Use your notes to write a paragraph about the animal you chose. Draw a picture for your paragraph.

9. Story to Song!
Working in a small group, turn the story *Mrs. Brown Went to Town* into a song. Choose one of your favorite songs. Change the words so that they tell the story of Mrs. Brown and her animals. Practice your song.

10. Weather Reporter
Predict the weather for each day of the school week. Take a piece of drawing paper and divide it into five columns. Draw pictures to show your predictions. For example, if you predict that Monday will be sunny, draw a sun. Imagine that you are a weather reporter on television. Present your weather report to the class.

Grade 2 Theme 1: Silly Stories   Activity Master CM 1–12

THEME 2/SELECTION 1: *Henry and Mudge and the Starry Night*

Assignments for Independent Activities

Assign for On-Level Students

Masters: CM 2-1—CM 2-4

Teacher support: GO-1, GO-2, GO-3, GO-4

Classroom materials: See list of materials with each activity.

Note: Many activities are appropriate for Extra Support students and English Language Learners.

Check that students have read the selection or leveled reading specified for an activity.

- Anthology, pp. 122-153: *Henry and Mudge and the Starry Night;* "Campfire Games"
- Phonics Library: *Miss Pig's Garden; Mike and Dave Sleep Outside*

Assign for Challenge Students

Masters: CH 2-1, CH 2-2

Teacher support: GO-1, GO-2

Classroom materials: Books of familiar children's songs, map of your state, encyclopedia, almanac

Note: Many activities are appropriate for advanced English Language Learners.

- Theme Paperbacks: *Animal Tracks Are Everywhere* (On My Way Practice Reader); *Amelia Bedelia Goes Camping* (On Level); *Chibi* (Challenge)

Provide copies of activity masters, graphic organizer masters, and challenge masters, as needed.

Additional Activities and Program Resources

Additional independent activities for this selection:

- Practice Book, pp. 72, 76, 77, 78, 80, 81, 82, 235
- Teacher's Resources Blackline Masters, Theme 2 Reading Cards 2, 3, 4
- TE pp. R5, R7, R15, R21, R29, R32
- TE Challenge pp. 115, 146, 152, 153, 153H, R5, R7, R15, R21, R29

Other program resources:

- Suggested in activities for this selection: Houghton Mifflin Science DiscoveryWorks Trade Books: *Mousekin's Lost Woodland*
- Students' self-selected independent reading materials
- Students' journals or other independent writing materials

Get Set to Read *Henry and Mudge and the Starry Night*

Education Place: www.eduplace.com for more activities related to *Henry and Mudge and the Starry Night*

Accelerated Reader®, *Henry and Mudge and the Starry Night*

Audiotape, *Henry and Mudge and the Starry Night*

Extra Support lessons for *Henry and Mudge and the Starry Night*

English language development lessons for *Henry and Mudge and the Starry Night*

DAY 1

Preteach Phonics: Long Vowels *o, u, e*
Preteach Two Sounds for *g*
Preview *Miss Pig's Garden*
• ES Handbook pp. 46–47 and masters PMES 2-1, TMES 2-1

Preteach The Night Sky
Preteach Teacher Read Aloud *The Big Dipper*
Preteach Phonics: Long Vowels CVCe: *o, u, e*
• ELL Handbook pp. 50–51 and master ELL 2-1

DAY 2

Preteach Compare and Contrast
Preview Selection, Segment 1
• ES Handbook pp. 48–49 and masters PMES 2-2, TMES 2-2

Preteach Camping
Preteach Get Set to Read; Anthology Selection
Reteach High-Frequency Words: *beautiful, even*
• ELL Handbook pp. 52–53

DAY 3

Reteach High-Frequency Words
Reteach Telling Sentences and Questions
Preview Selection, Segment 2
• ES Handbook pp. 50–51

Preteach Woodland Animals
Reteach Phonics Review: Long Vowels CVCe: *a, i*
Reteach High-Frequency Words: *quiet, straight, year*
• ELL Handbook pp. 54–55

DAY 4

Reteach Phonics: *o, u,* and *e* in CVCe patterns
Reteach Phonics: Two Sounds for *g*
Preview *Mike and Dave Sleep Outside*
• ES Handbook pp. 52–53

Preteach Musical Instruments
Reteach Selection Summary and Review
Reteach Vocabulary: Compound Words
• ELL Handbook pp. 56–57 and master ELL 2-2

DAY 5

Reteach Compare and Contrast
Revisit Selection, *Mike and Dave Sleep Outside*, and *Miss Pig's Garden*
• ES Handbook pp. 54–55

Preteach Bodies of Water
Reteach Grammar: Telling Sentences and Questions
Reteach Writing: Making Complete Sentences
• ELL Handbook pp. 58–59

Activities

Henry and Mudge and the Starry Night

DAY 1

1. The Big Dipper 30 MIN. INDIVIDUAL

Materials: black construction paper

Extend this activity by having children make the entire constellation *Ursa Major.* (Science)

2. Compound Match 30 MIN. INDIVIDUAL / PAIR

Materials: strips of paper

If necessary, review compound words with children.

English Language Learners Have children work in pairs.

Additional Activities

- Audio Tape, *Henry and Mudge and the Starry Night*
- Practice Book, p. 235, Spelling
- Technology: See p. 14.

DAY 2

3. My Favorite Place Outdoors 30 MIN. INDIVIDUAL / PAIR

Materials: posterboard, crayons, and markers

Have children brainstorm familiar outdoor places before they choose their favorite. Display posters on a class bulletin board.

4. Build a Tree House 30 MIN. INDIVIDUAL

Materials: drawing paper, crayons, and markers

Explain *tree house.* Display tree house drawings on a classroom bulletin board. (Art)

Additional Activities

- Practice Book, p. 72, Comprehension
- Practice Book, p. 76, Spelling
- Practice Book, p. 80, Grammar
- Technology: See p. 14.

DAY 3

5. My Outside Adventure 40 MIN. INDIVIDUAL / PAIR

Materials: drawing paper, crayons, and markers

Display drawings on a classroom bulletin board.

Activity Master CM 2–1

Activity Master CM 2–2

6. Postcard from the Outdoors 20 MIN. INDIVIDUAL

Materials: **index cards, crayons, markers, and sample postcards**

Show sample postcards to children as models. You may want to write the school's address on the board for everyone to copy.

English Language Learners Brainstorm with children kinds of messages shown on postcards.

Additional Activities
- Practice Book, p. 77, Spelling
- Technology: See p. 14.

DAY 4

7. Nature Connections 30 MIN. INDIVIDUAL / PAIR

If children are having trouble, brainstorm with them a list of action words.

8. Campfire Categories 30 MIN. INDIVIDUAL / PAIR

Materials: **Graphic Organizer Master 1**

Brainstorm with students things they need on a trip and things they find when they get there.

Additional Activities
- Practice Book, p. 78, Spelling
- Practice Book, p. 81, Grammar
- Technology: See p. 14.

DAY 5

9. From Here to There 20 MIN. INDIVIDUAL

Tell children they can use symbols, as in a map key, pictures, or word notations. You might want to display maps on a classroom bulletin board.

10. National Parks 40 MIN. INDIVIDUAL

Materials: **Graphic Organizer Master 2, encyclopedia, access to the Internet (optional)**

Direct children to the National Park Service website at http://www.nps.gov

Additional Activities
- Anthology, pp. 148-149, Responding
- Practice Book, p. 82, Grammar
- TE p. R5, R7, R15, R21, R29, R32
- Technology: See p. 14.

Activity Master CM 2–3

THEME 2/*Henry and Mudge and the Starry Night*

Name_____

6. Postcard from the Outdoors
Imagine you have gone camping with your family in the woods, just like Henry and Mudge. Send a postcard to your class about your trip.
- Use an oaktag card to make your postcard. Draw a picture of something you saw while camping on one side of the card.
- Write a message to your class on the other side. In your message, explain the picture on the front side of the card.
- Sign your name after the message.

7. Nature Connections
Henry "ran like the wind" in the story *Henry and Mudge and the Starry Night*. What does it mean to "run like the wind"? Talk about it with a classmate. Then play Nature Connections.
- Write action words. For example: *sing, jump,* and *fall*.
- Invent phrases using the word *like*. The first word of the phrase must be an action word. The last word must be a word for something in nature. For example, *sing like a bird, jump like a kangaroo,* and *fall like rain*.
- Take turns with your classmate saying the phrases.

CM 2–3 Activity Master   Grade 2   Theme 2: Nature Walk

Activity Master CM 2–4

THEME 2/*Henry and Mudge and the Starry Night*

Name_____

8. Campfire Categories
What kinds of things do you need on a camping trip? What kinds of things do you find when you get there? Make two webs, one for things you need and one for things you find. Use things from the story *Henry and Mudge and the Starry Night* to help you fill in your webs. Share your webs with a classmate.

9. From Here to There
Imagine you are taking a walk from your classroom to another place in your school.
- Choose a place where you want to go. Think of the best way to get there from your classroom.
- Draw a map of the path from your classroom to this place.
- Add words or pictures of things you see along the way.
Show and explain your map to the class.

10. National Parks
Henry and his family go camping. A popular place for people to camp is a National Park. The United States has several national parks all over the country. Use a Venn diagram like the one on page 71 of the Practice Book to compare and contrast two national parks in the United States. First, choose two national parks. You can look them up in an encyclopedia or on the national park website. Think about what is the same and what is different about the parks you choose. Use that information to complete the Venn diagram.

Grade 2   Theme 2: Nature Walk   Activity Master **CM 2–4**

ASSIGNMENT PLANNER

THEME 2/SELECTION 2: *Exploring Parks with Ranger Dockett*

Assignments for Independent Activities

Assign for On-Level Students

Masters: CM 2-5—CM 2-8

Teacher support: GO-1, GO-2, GO-3, GO-4

Classroom materials: Poster board, crayons, markers, drawing paper, small index cards, large drawing paper

Note: Many activities are appropriate for **Extra Support** students and **English Language Learners.**

Assign for Challenge Students

Masters: CH 2-3, CH 2-4

Teacher support: GO-1, GO-2

Classroom materials: Drawing paper, crayons, markers, index cards, encyclopedia

Note: Many activities are appropriate for advanced English Language Learners.

Check that students have read the selection or leveled reading specified for an activity.

- Anthology, pp. 158–177: *Exploring Parks with Ranger Dockett;* "Nature Poems"

- Phonics Library: *A Trip to Central Park; Zeke and Pete Rule!*

- Theme Paperbacks: *Animal Tracks Are Everywhere* (On My Way Practice Reader); *Amelia Bedelia Goes Camping* (On Level); *Chibi* (Challenge)

Provide copies of activity masters, graphic organizer masters, and challenge masters, as needed.

Additional Activities and Program Resources

Additional independent activities for this selection:

- Practice Book, pp. 95, 99, 100, 101, 103, 104, 105, 235

- Teacher's Resources Blackline Masters, Theme 2 Reading Cards 6, 7, 8

- TE pp. R9, R11, R17, R23, R30, R32

- TE Challenge pp. 174, 177, 177H, 178G, R9, R11, R17, R23, R30

Other program resources:

- Suggested in activities for this selection: Houghton Mifflin Science DiscoveryWorks Trade Books: *Mousekin's Lost Woodland*

- Students' self-selected independent reading materials

- Students' journals or other independent writing materials

Technology

Get Set to Read *Exploring Parks with Ranger Dockett*

Education Place: www.eduplace.com for more activities related to *Exploring Parks with Ranger Dockett*

Accelerated Reader®, *Exploring Parks with Ranger Dockett*

Audiotape, *Exploring Parks with Ranger Dockett*

Extra Support lessons for _Exploring Parks with Ranger Dockett_

English language development lessons for _Exploring Parks with Ranger Dockett_

DAY 1

Preteach Phonics: Consonant Clusters (*r, l, s*)

Preteach Phonics: Two Sounds for *c*

Preview *A Trip to Central Park*

- ES Handbook pp. 56–57 and masters PMES 2–3, TMES 2–3

Preteach Park Rules

Preteach Teacher Read Aloud *A Moose in the Bathroom*

Preteach Phonics: Consonant Clusters (*r, l, s*)

- ELL Handbook pp. 60–61 and master ELL 2–4

DAY 2

Preteach Fact and Opinion

Preview Selection, Segment 1

- ES Handbook pp. 58–59 and masters PMES 2–4, TMES 2–4

Preteach Things in a Park

Preteach Get Set to Read; Anthology Selection

Reteach High-Frequency Words: *busy, important*

- ELL Handbook pp. 62–63

DAY 3

Reteach High-Frequency Words

Reteach Commands

Preview Selection, Segment 2

- ES Handbook pp. 60–61

Preteach Ponds

Reteach Phonics Review: Long Vowels CVCe: *o, u, e*

Reteach High-Frequency Words: *later, touch, young*

- ELL Handbook pp. 64–65

DAY 4

Reteach Phonics: Consonant Clusters (*r, l, s*)

Reteach Phonics: Two Sounds for *c*

Preview *Zeke and Pete Rule!*

- ES Handbook pp. 62–63

Preteach Animals in a Park

Reteach Selection Summary and Review

Reteach Vocabulary: Antonyms

- ELL Handbook pp. 66–67 and master ELL 2–5

DAY 5

Reteach Fact and Opinion

Revisit Selection, *A Trip to Central Park*, and *Zeke and Pete Rule!*

- ES Handbook pp. 64–65

Preteach Community Helpers

Reteach Grammar: Commands

Reteach Writing: Main Idea and Details

- ELL Handbook pp. 68–69

Activities

Exploring Parks with Ranger Dockett

Activity Master CM 2–5

THEME 2/*Exploring Parks with Ranger Dockett*

Name_____

1. What Am I Thinking Of?
In this game, your partner must guess what you are describing from a picture in *Exploring Parks with Ranger Dockett*.
- Choose a picture from the story.
- Choose an item in the picture to describe to your partner. Do not tell your partner what the item is.
- Using descriptive words, tell your partner about the item.
- See if you partner can guess the item.
- Switch roles and let your partner describe an item to you.

2. Park Statue
Look at the photographs of the different statues in Ranger Dockett's park. Make another statue for his park.
- Think about something that could be a statue.
- Draw a picture of your statue and paste your drawing to a piece of poster board.
- Write two or three sentences explaining why the statue would be a nice addition to the park. Write a sentence telling where in the park you would put the statue.

3. *Animal Tracks Are Everywhere/Amelia Bedelia Goes Camping*
Read the story *Animal Tracks Are Everywhere* or *Amelia Bedelia Goes Camping*. Then fill in a story map using information from the story. Tell the story to a classmate in your own words, using the notes from your chart.

CM 2–5 Activity Master   Grade 2   Theme 2: Nature Walk

Activity Master CM 2–6

THEME 2/*Exploring Parks with Ranger Dockett*

Name_____

4. Animal Squares
Play a game of animal squares with a classmate.
- Draw a large chart with five columns and five rows.
- At the top of each colum, write a letter of the alphabet.
- Fill in the rows with the names of animals that begin with each letter.
- Play again using different letters.

5. Park Adventures
Make up stories about adventures in a park with a small group of your classmates.
- One person in the group begins the story by naming a character and an event.
- Each member of the group adds one event to the story. All events must be about the character.
- The last person in the group must end the story.
- Then a different member of the group begins a new story. Everyone in the group should begin and end a new story.

6. Earth Day
Every year people all over the world celebrate Earth Day. On that day people do good things for nature. Make an Earth Day poster. Think of five things your class can do on Earth Day. Write them on the poster. Add drawings and photographs. Give your poster a title. Display your poster and read your ideas to a classmate.

Grade 2   Theme 2: Nature Walk   Activity Master CM 2–6

1. What Am I Thinking Of? 40 MIN. INDIVIDUAL / PAIR
Tell children to use vivid details to create a clear image for their partners.

2. Park Statue 30 MIN. INDIVIDUAL
Materials: poster board, crayons, and markers

Have children look at the pictures of statues in the story before they make their own. Display children's posters on a class bulletin board.

Additional Activities
- Audio Tape, *Exploring Parks with Ranger Dockett*
- Practice Book, p. 235, Spelling
- Technology: See p. 18.

3. *Animal Tracks Are Everywhere* (On My Way Practice Reader)/*Amelia Bedelia Goes Camping* (On-Level Theme Paperback) 30 MIN. INDIVIDUAL
Materials: Graphic Organizer Master 3

Tell children it will be helpful to fill in the chart as they read.

English Language Learners Have children work in pairs and take turns reading the story out loud.

4. Animal Squares 30 MIN. PAIR
Materials: drawing paper

Check to make sure children understand how to make the game board. Make sure the squares in the game board are large enough for writing.

English Language Learners Have children use a dictionary to check spelling and an encyclopedia to find pictures of unfamiliar animals.

Additional Activities
- Practice Book, p. 95, Comprehension
- Practice Book, p. 99, Spelling
- Practice Book, p. 103, Grammar
- Technology: See p. 18.

5. Park Adventures 30 MIN. SMALL GROUP
Have children pick their group's favorite story and tell it to the whole class.

6. Earth Day   30 MIN.   INDIVIDUAL / PAIR

Give examples of Earth Day events in your community. You might want to choose an idea from the poster and make it a class project. (Social Studies) (Science)

Additional Activities
- Practice Book, p. 100, Spelling
- Technology: See p. 18.

DAY 4

7. Pet Survey   30 MIN.   INDIVIDUAL

Talk with children about how surveys help people gather information.

English Language Learners Pair children with others to help them spell pet names. Have them check their spelling with a dictionary.

8. My Garden   30 MIN.   INDIVIDUAL / PAIR
Materials: small index cards, large drawing paper, crayons, and markers

Talk about how a garden provides green spaces and animal habitat. Explain that landscapers use garden symbols to design a garden in the same way that the children are doing when they arrange their cards.

Additional Activities
- Practice Book, p. 101, Spelling
- Practice Book, p. 104, Grammar
- Practice Book, p. 104, Grammar
- Technology: See p. 18.

DAY 5

9. Park Poem   30 MIN.   INDIVIDUAL

You might want to collect all the poems and create a class poem book.

English Language Learners: Pair children with fluent English speakers.

10. Fact or Opinion?   30 MIN.   INDIVIDUAL
Materials: Graphic Organizer Master 4

If necessary, review a K-W-L chart and the difference between fact and opinion with children.

Additional Activities
- Anthology, pp. 174–175, Responding
- Practice Book, p. 105, Grammar
- TE p. R9, R11, R17, R23, R30, R32
- Technology: See p. 18.

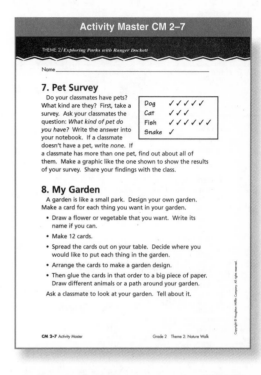

Activity Master CM 2–7

THEME 2 / *Exploring Parks with Ranger Dockett*

Name

7. Pet Survey
Do your classmates have pets? What kind are they? First, take a survey. Ask your classmates the question: *What kind of pet do you have?* Write the answer into your notebook. If a classmate doesn't have a pet, write *none*. If a classmate has more than one pet, find out about all of them. Make a graphic like the one shown to show the results of your survey. Share your findings with the class.

Dog	✓ ✓ ✓ ✓ ✓
Cat	✓ ✓ ✓
Fish	✓ ✓ ✓ ✓ ✓ ✓
Snake	✓

8. My Garden
A garden is like a small park. Design your own garden. Make a card for each thing you want in your garden.
- Draw a flower or vegetable that you want. Write its name if you can.
- Make 12 cards.
- Spread the cards out on your table. Decide where you would like to put each thing in the garden.
- Arrange the cards to make a garden design.
- Then glue the cards in that order to a big piece of paper. Draw different animals or a path around your garden.

Ask a classmate to look at your garden. Tell about it.

CM 2–7 Activity Master   Grade 2   Theme 2: Nature Walk

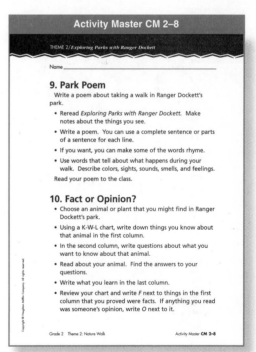

Activity Master CM 2–8

THEME 2 / *Exploring Parks with Ranger Dockett*

Name

9. Park Poem
Write a poem about taking a walk in Ranger Dockett's park.
- Reread *Exploring Parks with Ranger Dockett.* Make notes about the things you see.
- Write a poem. You can use a complete sentence or parts of a sentence for each line.
- If you want, you can make some of the words rhyme.
- Use words that tell about what happens during your walk. Describe colors, sights, sounds, smells, and feelings.

Read your poem to the class.

10. Fact or Opinion?
- Choose an animal or plant that you might find in Ranger Dockett's park.
- Using a K-W-L chart, write down things you know about that animal in the first column.
- In the second column, write questions about what you want to know about that animal.
- Read about your animal. Find the answers to your questions.
- Write what you learn in the last column.
- Review your chart and write *F* next to things in the first column that you proved were facts. If anything you read was someone's opinion, write *O* next to it.

Grade 2   Theme 2: Nature Walk   Activity Master **CM 2–8**

THEME 2/SELECTION 3: *Around the Pond: Who's Been Here?*

Assignments for Independent Activities

Assign for On-Level Students

Masters: CM 2-9—CM 2-12

Teacher support: GO-1, GO-2, GO-3, GO-4

Classroom materials: See list of materials with each activity.

Note: Many activities are appropriate for Extra Support students and English Language Learners.

Assign for Challenge Students

Masters: CH 2-5, CH 2-6

Teacher support: GO-1, GO-2

Classroom materials: See list of materials with each activity.

Note: Many activities are appropriate for advanced English Language Learners.

Check that students have read the selection or leveled reading specified for an activity.

- Anthology, pp. 180–209: *Around the Pond: Who's Been Here?;* "How to Be a Wildlife Spy"
- Phonics Library: *In the Woods; A Snake Sheds Its Skin*

- Theme Paperbacks: *Animal Tracks Are Everywhere* (On My Way Practice Reader); *Amelia Bedelia Goes Camping* (On Level); *Chibi* (Challenge)

Provide copies of activity masters, graphic organizer masters, and challenge masters, as needed.

Additional Activities and Program Resources

Additional independent activities for this selection:

- Practice Book, pp. 108, 112, 115, 116, 117, 118, 120, 121, 122, 239
- Teacher's Resources Blackline Masters, Theme 2 Reading Cards 10, 11
- TE pp. R13, R19, R25, R31, R33
- TE Challenge pp. 202, 209, 211, R13, R19, R25, R30, R31, R33

Other program resources:

- Suggested in activities for this selection: Houghton Mifflin Science DiscoveryWorks Trade Books: *Mousekin's Lost Woodland*
- Students' self-selected independent reading materials
- Students' journals or other independent writing materials

Get Set to Read *Around the Pond: Who's Been Here?*

Education Place: www.eduplace.com for more activities related to *Around the Pond: Who's Been Here?*

Accelerated Reader®, *Around the Pond: Who's Been Here?*

Audiotape, *Around the Pond: Who's Been Here?*

Extra Support lessons for *Around the Pond: Who's Been Here?*

English language development lessons for *Around the Pond: Who's Been Here?*

DAY 1

Preteach Phonics: Double Final Consonants
Review Phonics: VCCV: Double Consonants
Preview *In the Woods*
- ES Handbook pp. 66–67 and masters PMES 2-5, TMES 2-5

Preteach Words That Show Position
Preteach Teacher Read Aloud *Squirrels and Chipmunks*
Preteach Phonics: Double Consonants
- ELL Handbook pp. 70–71 and master ELL 2-7

DAY 2

Preteach Categorize and Classify
Preview Selection, Segment 1
- ES Handbook pp. 68–69 and masters PMES 2-6, TMES 2-6

Preteach Weather
Preteach Get Set to Read; Anthology Selection
Reteach High-Frequency Words: *brother, great*
- ELL Handbook pp. 72–73

DAY 3

Reteach High-Frequency Words
Reteach Exclamations
Preview Selection, Segment 2
- ES Handbook pp. 70–71

Preteach Things You Do in Water
Reteach Phonics Review: Consonant Clusters *(r, l, s)*
Reteach High-Frequency Words: *across, stand*
- ELL Handbook pp. 74–75

DAY 4

Reteach Phonics: Double Final Consonants
Reteach VCCV Pattern
Preview *A Snake Sheds Its Skin*
- ES Handbook pp. 72–73

Preteach Pets
Reteach Selection Summary and Review
Reteach Vocabulary: Multiple-Meaning Words
- ELL Handbook pp. 76–77 and ELL 2-8

DAY 5

Reteach Categorize and Classify
Revisit Selection, *In the Woods*, and *A Snake Sheds Its Skin*
- ES Handbook pp. 74–75

Preteach Fruit
Reteach Grammar: Exclamations
Reteach Writing: Telling More
- ELL Handbook pp. 78–79

Activities

SELECTION 3:
Around the Pond: Who's Been Here?

Activity Master CM 2–9

THEME 2/*Around the Pond: Who's Been Here?*

Name_____

1. Colorful Words
The children pick blueberries in the story *Around the Pond: Who's Been Here?* The word *blueberry* is a compound word. It is made up of two words: *blue* and *berry*. How many compound words with colors do you know?

• Make a chart with six columns.
• Label the columns: *black*, *blue*, *red*, and *white*. Add two more colors to your chart.
• Write compound words that you already know.
• Look up more words in a dictionary. Complete your chart with as many colorful words as you can.

Make up sentences with a classmate. Use each of your compound words in a sentence.

2. Animal Descriptions
Play this animal game with a classmate.

• Write words that describe how animals look. For example: *tail*, *fur*, and *claws*.
• Choose words from the list and write one word on each card. Make at least six cards.
• Divide the cards between you and your classmate.
• On the back of the card, write the names of animals that fit the category on the front of the card.

Look over the completed cards. Talk about how the animals are the same or different.

CM 2–9 Activity Master   Grade 2 Theme 2: Nature Walk

Activity Master CM 2–10

THEME 2/*Around the Pond: Who's Been Here?*

Name_____

3. Wow!
You have learned that an exclamation is a sentence that shows strong feeling, such as surprise or fear. It ends with an exclamation point. Look at the pictures of the animals in *Around the Pond: Who's Been There?* Write two exclamation sentences or words for each animal picture. For example: *What a long neck! Look at the bright colors!*

Show the picture of the animal and read your exclamations to the class.

4. Nature Puzzle
A picture puzzle is a picture that is cut up into pieces. Make a puzzle and see if a classmate can solve it.

• Paint that scene on a piece of drawing paper. Include details, such as animals and plants.
• Be sure your scene is clearly drawn so that when you cut it, you can remember how it should look.
• Let the picture dry. Fold the paper four times. Cut the picture into squares along the folds.
• Mix the squares up. These are your puzzle pieces.

Give the squares to classmates. Can they solve the puzzle?

5. Life Cycles
Choose an animal from *Around the Pond: Who's Been Here?* and find the steps in its life cycle. Use what you learn to make a diagram that shows its life cycle.

Grade 2 Theme 2: Nature Walk   Activity Master **CM 2–10**

DAY 1

1. Colorful Words   30 MIN.   INDIVIDUAL / PAIR
Materials: dictionary

Explain compound words. Tell children that the color word can be the first or last part of a compound word.

2. Animal Descriptions   30 MIN.   INDIVIDUAL / PAIR
Materials: dictionary and books about animals

Brainstorm with children some of the characteristics of animals.

> **Additional Activities**
>
> • Audio Tape, *Around the Pond: Who's Been Here?*
> • Practice Book, p. 108, Phonics
> • Practice Book, p. 239, Spelling
> • Technology: See p. 22.

DAY 2

3. Wow!   20 MIN.   INDIVIDUAL / PAIR

Give examples of exclamations. Explain how they are used to express feelings or a personal point of view.

English Language Learners Pair children with other children who are more fluent in English.

4. Nature Puzzle   60 MIN.   INDIVIDUAL / PAIR
Materials: drawing paper, brushes, paint, and scissors

Show a picture puzzle to the class or illustrate it on the chalkboard. Tell children to paint detailed pictures. (Art)

> **Additional Activities**
>
> • Practice Book, p. 112, Comprehension
> • Practice Book, p. 116, Spelling
> • Practice Book, p. 120, Grammar
> • Technology: See p. 22.

DAY 3

5. Life Cycles   30 MIN.   INDIVIDUAL / SMALL GROUP
Materials: large drawing paper, crayons, and markers

Tell children that their diagrams should have a circle for each step. Display diagrams on a classroom bulletin board. Children can use their science textbook for information about life cycles.

6. Wildlife Collage <u>30 MIN.</u> INDIVIDUAL / PAIR

Materials: *construction paper, old magazines, scissors, and glue*

Display collages on a classroom bulletin board. (Science) (Art)

English Language Learners Review *collage* with children. Have them work in pairs.

> ### Additional Activities
> • Practice Book, p. 117, Spelling   • Technology: See p. 22.

DAY 4

7. Naturalists <u>40 MIN.</u> INDIVIDUAL

Materials: *encyclopedia and other references sources, crayons, and markers*

Ask volunteers to share their reports with the class.

8. What Do You See? <u>20 MIN.</u> SMALL GROUP

Explain why it is important to note details and keep these details in your head for this activity.

English Language Learners Have children play the game in pairs.

> ### Additional Activities
> • Practice Book, p. 115, Phonics   • Practice Book, p. 121, Grammar
> • Practice Book, p. 118, Spelling   • Technology: See p. 22.

DAY 5

9. Thumbprint Detective <u>40 MIN.</u> INDIVIDUAL / SMALL GROUP
Materials: *inked stamp pad, index cards and paper towels*

Talk about how fingerprints are unique to an individual. Explain how and why fingerprinting is useful.

10. Puppet Show <u>40 MIN.</u> SMALL GROUP
Materials: *stiff paper, masking tape, craft sticks, crayons, and markers*

Remind children that they are acting out the puppet show from the point of view of the animals. Ask volunteers to perform their puppet shows.

> ### Additional Activities
> • Anthology, pp. 204–205,   • TE p. R13, R19, R25, R31, R33
>   Responding   • Technology: See p.22.
> • Practice Book, p. 122, Grammar

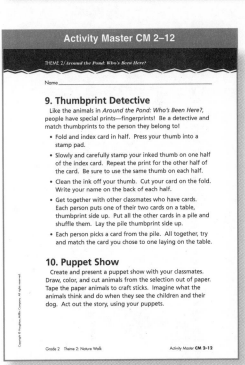

ASSIGNMENT PLANNER

THEME 3/SELECTION 1: *Chinatown*

Assignments for Independent Activities

Assign for On-Level Students

Masters: CM 3-1—CM 3-4

Teacher support: GO-1, GO-3

Classroom materials: Small paper bags, drawing paper, construction paper, crayons, markers, a ruler

Note: Many activities are appropriate for Extra Support students and English Language Learners.

Assign for Challenge Students

Masters: CH 3-1, CH 3-2

Teacher support: GO-1, GO-5

Classroom materials: Encyclopedia, drawing paper, crayons, markers, art paper, colored construction paper, glue

Note: Many activities are appropriate for advanced English Language Learners.

Check that students have read the selection or leveled reading specified for an activity.

- Anthology, pp. 234-263: *Chinatown;* "Make a Tangram"

- Phonics Library: *Sunshine for the Circus; Mother's Day Parade on Park Street*

- Theme Paperbacks: *Catching Bailey* (On My Way Practice Reader); *Harry's Pony* (On Level); *Solo Girl* (Challenge)

Provide copies of activity masters, graphic organizer masters, and challenge masters, as needed.

Additional Activities and Program Resources

Additional independent activities for this selection:

- Practice Book, pp. 136, 140, 144, 145, 146, 148, 149, 150, 241

- Teacher's Resources Blackline Masters, Theme 3 Reading Cards 2, 3

- TE pp. R5, R7, R21, R29, R40, R42

- TE Challenge pp. 227, 256, 263, 263H, R5, R7, R21, R29, R40

Other program resources:

- Suggested in activities for this selection: Houghton Mifflin Social Studies Bookshelf: *City Green*

- Students' self-selected independent reading materials

- Students' journals or other independent writing materials

Get Set to Read *Chinatown*

Education Place: www.eduplace.com for more activities related to *Chinatown*

Accelerated Reader®, *Chinatown*

Audiotape, *Chinatown*

Extra Support lessons for *Chinatown*

English language development lessons for *Chinatown*

DAY 1

Preteach Phonics: Consonant Digraphs *sh, ch*
Preteach Base Words and Endings *-er* and *-est*
Preview *Sunshine for the Circus*
- ES Handbook pp. 78–79 and masters PMES 3-1, TMES 3-1

Preteach Types of Homes
Preteach Teacher Read Aloud *Good-bye, Curtis*
Preteach Phonics: Consonant Digraphs *th, wh, sh, ch (tch)*
- ELL Handbook pp. 82–83 and master ELL 3-1

DAY 2

Preteach Making Judgments
Preview Selection, Segment 1
- ES Handbook pp. 80–81 and masters PMES 3-2, TMES 3-2

Preteach Types of Shops
Preteach Get Set to Read; Anthology Selection
Reteach High-Frequency Words: *during, heard*
- ELL Handbook pp. 84–85

DAY 3

Reteach High-Frequency Words
Reteach Naming Words (Common Nouns)
Preview Selection, Segment 2
- ES Handbook pp. 82–83

Preteach Types of Restaurants
Reteach Phonics Review: Double Consonants; High-Frequency Words: *lion, winter*
- ELL Handbook pp. 86–87

DAY 4

Reteach Phonics: Consonant Digraphs *th, wh, sh, ch (tch)*
Reteach Base Words and Endings *-er, -est*
Preview *Mother's Day Parade on Park Street*
- ES Handbook pp. 84–85

Preteach Exercise
Reteach Selection Summary and Review
Reteach Vocabulary/Dictionary: ABC Order to the Third Letter
- ELL Handbook pp. 88–89 and master ELL 3-2

DAY 5

Reteach Making Judgments
Revisit Selection, *Mother's Day Parade on Park Street*, and *Sunshine for the Circus*
- ES Handbook pp. 86–87

Preteach Holidays
Reteach Grammar: Naming Words (Common Nouns); Writing: Using Exact Words
- ELL Handbook pp. 90–91

Activity Master CM 3–1

THEME 3/*Chinatown*

Name _____

1. New Year Resolutions

The start of a new year is a time when people make *resolutions*, or decisions to make changes in their lives. Make your own list of resolutions. Think about

- new activities you want to try
- new ways to act and do things

Write ten resolutions and number them. For example:

1. *I will read more books.*
2. *I will be nicer to my brother.*

Read and explain your list to a classmate.

2. *Mother's Day Parade on Park Street*

Reread the story *Mother's Day Parade on Park Street*. Then make a chart to tell what you liked and what you didn't like about the story. Your chart should look like this:

What I Liked	What I Didn't Like	Reasons Why I Feel This Way

With a classmate, talk about the things listed in your chart.

CM 3–1 Activity Master   Grade 2   Theme 3: Around Town: Neighborhood and Community

---

Activity Master CM 3–2

THEME 3/*Chinatown*

Name _____

3. Paper Bag Story

Create a surprise story about things in your neighborhood.

- Tear or cut 12 strips of paper. Write one word on each strip.
- Six of the words must name a place, person, or thing in your neighborhood.
- Six of the words must be action verbs.

Get together with classmates. Put your words into a paper bag. Follow these steps to tell a story:

- Take one strip of paper out of the bag at a time.
- Use the word in a sentence to begin the story. Don't put the strip of paper back in the bag.
- The next person continues the story by picking a word out of the bag and using it in a sentence.
- Continue the story until there are no more strips of paper.

4. Neighborhood Flag

Make a flag for your neighborhood to display during an important celebration.

- Use colors that tell about your neighborhood. For example, green might show that there are lots of trees.
- Use shapes or objects that you see in your neighborhood. For example, draw a sun if it's usually sunny or draw a special bird that lives there.

Draw the flag and show it to a classmate. Explain the colors, shapes, and objects.

Grade 2   Theme 3: Around Town: Neighborhood and Community   Activity Master CM 3–2

DAY 1

1. New Year Resolutions   30 MIN.   INDIVIDUAL / SMALL GROUP

Explain *resolutions*. Give examples of sentences in the future tense. Create a class resolution list using examples from the children's lists.

English Language Learners Have children use a dictionary to find the spelling and meaning of words.

2. *Mother's Day Parade on Park Street*
(Phonics Library)   30 MIN.   INDIVIDUAL / PAIR

Tell children it might help them to brainstorm a list of things they liked and disliked before making their charts.

Additional Activities

- Audio Tape, *Chinatown*
- Practice Book, p. 136, Phonics
- Practice Book, p. 24, Spelling
- Technology: See p. 26.

DAY 2

3. Paper Bag Story   40 MIN.   SMALL GROUP

Materials: small paper bags

Instruct children to invent a story with a beginning, middle, and end. Make sure everyone takes turns adding sentences. The game can be played more than once.

English Language Learners Place children in a group with children who are more fluent in English.

4. Neighborhood Flag   20 MIN.   INDIVIDUAL

Materials: drawing paper, construction paper, crayons, and markers

Show the American flag to children and explain the meaning of the stars and stripes. (Social Studies)

Additional Activities

- Practice Book, p. 140, Comprehension
- Practice Book, p. 144, Spelling
- Practice Book, p. 148, Grammar
- Technology: See p.26.

DAY 3

5. What Happens Next?   40 MIN.   INDIVIDUAL / PAIR

Make sure that children understand that the shopping trip ends on page

249 in the story *Chinatown*. What happens next in the story tells of events from a different time period. Children must create a story that concludes the day after the shopping trip.

6. Fun in the Neighborhood   30 MIN.   INDIVIDUAL / PAIR
Ask volunteers to share their events with the class.

Additional Activities
- Practice Book, p. 145, Spelling
- Technology: See p. 26.

DAY 4

7. Plan a Parade   30 MIN.   INDIVIDUAL / PAIR
Materials: *drawing paper, markers, and a ruler*

Provide children with a simple street map as a model for this activity. (Social Studies)

8. My Favorite Place   20 MIN.   INDIVIDUAL
Materials: *drawing paper and markers*

Tell children to provide details and give reasons why it's their favorite place.

Additional Activities
- Practice Book, p. 146, Spelling
- Practice Book, p. 149, Grammar
- Technology: See p. 26.

DAY 5

9. Hopscotch   40 MIN.   INDIVIDUAL / PAIR
Materials: *drawing paper and markers*

Have children demonstrate how to play their game of hopscotch.

10. Card for My Neighborhood   20 MIN.   INDIVIDUAL
Materials: *construction paper, crayons, and markers*

Have children brainstorm a list of things they like about their neighborhood as a basis for their poem. (Social Studies)

English Language Learners Have children use a dictionary to check spelling and meaning of words.

Additional Activities
- Anthology, pp. 258–259, Responding
- Practice Book, p. 150, Grammar
- TE p. R5, R7, R21, R29, R40, R42
- Technology: See p. 26.

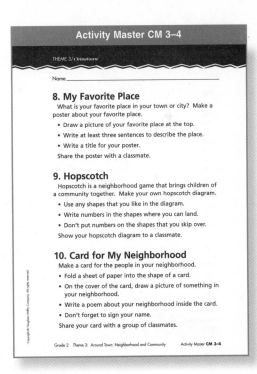

Activity Master CM 3–3

THEME 3/*Chinatown*

Name_____

5. What Happens Next?
What did the boy do after he finished shopping in *Chinatown*? The author doesn't tell us.
Look at the pictures on pages 234–249. Imagine what the boy does after that. Write a story about what happens. Write at least 12 sentences.
Compare your story with a classmate's story. Did you imagine the same events as your classmate?

6. Fun in the Neighborhood
Plan a special event for your neighborhood. Think about the best time of year for the event. What can everyone do together during this time of the year? Make a list of different events. Write a paragraph about the event you chose. Compare your idea with a classmate's idea. What is alike or different about them?

7. Plan a Parade
You are in charge of planning a neighborhood parade. Draw a map of your neighborhood. Show and label streets and buildings on the map. Look at your map and think about where the parade will start and end. Plan the best way for the parade to go from start to finish. Show the map to a classmate and describe your plan.

CM 3–3 Activity Master   Grade 2   Theme 3: Around Town: Neighborhood and Community

Activity Master CM 3–4

THEME 3/*Chinatown*

Name_____

8. My Favorite Place
What is your favorite place in your town or city? Make a poster about your favorite place.
- Draw a picture of your favorite place at the top.
- Write at least three sentences to describe the place.
- Write a title for your poster.
Share the poster with a classmate.

9. Hopscotch
Hopscotch is a neighborhood game that brings children of a community together. Make your own hopscotch diagram.
- Use any shapes that you like in the diagram.
- Write numbers in the shapes where you can land.
- Don't put numbers on the shapes that you skip over.
Show your hopscotch diagram to a classmate.

10. Card for My Neighborhood
Make a card for the people in your neighborhood.
- Fold a sheet of paper into the shape of a card.
- On the cover of the card, draw a picture of something in your neighborhood.
- Write a poem about your neighborhood inside the card.
- Don't forget to sign your name.
Share your card with a group of classmates.

Grade 2   Theme 3: Around Town: Neighborhood and Community   Activity Master **CM 3–4**

THEME 3/SELECTION 2: *A Trip to the Firehouse*

Assignments for Independent Activities

Assign for On-Level Students

Masters: CM 3-5—CM 3-8

Teacher support: GO-1, GO-3

Classroom materials: Index cards, drawing paper, crayons, markers, photocopies of Transparency 3-R

Note: Many activities are appropriate for Extra Support students and English Language Learners.

Assign for Challenge Students

Masters: CH 3-3, CH 3-4

Teacher support: GO-1, GO-5

Classroom materials: Poster board, crayons, markers, drawing paper

Note: Many activities are appropriate for advanced English Language Learners.

Check that students have read the selection or leveled reading specified for an activity.

- Anthology, pp. 268–295: *A Trip to the Firehouse;* "Fire-Safety Tips"

- Phonics Library: *Jay the Mailman; Watch Out for Thick Mud!*

- Theme Paperbacks: *Catching Bailey* (On My Way Practice Reader); *Harry's Pony* (On Level); *Solo Girl* (Challenge)

Provide copies of activity masters, graphic organizer masters, and challenge masters, as needed.

Additional Activities and Program Resources

Additional independent activities for this selection:

- Practice Book, pp. 163, 167, 168, 169, 171, 172, 173, 243

- Teacher's Resources Blackline Masters, Theme 3 Reading Cards 5, 6

- TE pp. R9, R11, R23, R31, R40, R42

- TE Challenge pp. 288, 295, 295H, R9, R11, R23, R31, R40

Other program resources:

- Suggested in activities for this selection: Houghton Mifflin Social Studies Bookshelf: *City Green*

- Students' self-selected independent reading materials

- Students' journals or other independent writing materials

Get Set to Read *A Trip to the Firehouse*

Education Place: www.eduplace.com for more activities related to *A Trip to the Firehouse*

Accelerated Reader®, *A Trip to the Firehouse*

Audiotape, *A Trip to the Firehouse*

Extra Support lessons for *A Trip to the Firehouse*

English language development lessons for *A Trip to the Firehouse*

DAY 1

Preteach Phonics: Vowel Pairs *ai, ay*

Preteach Compound Words

Preview *Jay and the Mailman*

- ES Handbook pp. 88–89 and masters PMES 3–3, TMES 3–3

Preteach Things on a Street

Preteach Teacher Read Aloud *A Seldom-Seen Neighbor*

Preteach Phonics: Vowel Pairs *ai, ay*

- ELL Handbook pp. 92–93 and master ELL 3–4

DAY 2

Preteach Topic, Main Idea, Details

Preview Selection, Segment 1

- ES Handbook pp. 90–91 and masters PMES 3–4, TMES 3–4

Preteach Neighborhood Buildings

Preteach Get Set to Read; Anthology Selection

Reteach High-Frequency Words: *clothes, guess*

- ELL Handbook pp. 94–95

DAY 3

Reteach High-Frequency Words

Reteach Special Nouns (Proper Nouns)

Preview Selection, Segment 2

- ES Handbook pp. 92–93

Preteach Vehicles

Reteach Phonics Review: Consonant Digraphs *th, wh, sh, ch (tch)*; High-Frequency Word: *order*

- ELL Handbook pp. 96–97

DAY 4

Reteach Phonics: Vowel Pairs *ai, ay*

Reteach Compound Words

Preview *Watch Out for Thick Mud!*

- ES Handbook pp. 94–95

Preteach Emergencies

Reteach Selection Summary and Review

Reteach Vocabulary/Dictionary: Beginning, Middle, End

- ELL Handbook pp. 98–99 and master ELL 3–5

DAY 5

Reteach Topic, Main Idea, Details

Revisit Selection, *Jay and the Mailman*, and *Watch Out for Thick Mud!*

- ES Handbook pp. 96–97

Preteach Time

Reteach Grammar: Special Nouns; Writing: Choosing What Is Important

- ELL Handbook pp. 100–101

Activity Master CM 3–5

Name _____

1. Pretend Pets
Spot is the name of the pet dog in *A Trip to the Firehouse*. Why is Spot a good name? Think of an animal you would like as a pet. What name would you give it and why?

- Draw a picture of your favorite kind of animal.
- Give your pretend pet a name.
- Write the main idea and details that tell why the name is a good one for your pretend pet. For example: *Main Idea: Scruffy is a good name for my pet. Details: He has a lot of fur. The fur is always a mess.*

Tell a classmate about your pretend pet and its name.

2. Firefighter Interview
In the story you learn a lot about the jobs of firefighters. With a partner, act out an interview. Each of you should prepare questions you would like to ask a firefighter. Then, one of you plays the interviewer and one of you plays the firefighter. Switch roles and interview again.

3. *Catching Bailey/Harry's Pony*
Read the story *Catching Bailey* or *Harry's Pony*. Use a story map to show the characters, setting, and events at the beginning, middle, and end of the story. Share your map with a classmate who read the same story. Talk about what happened in the story.

Activity Master CM 3–6

Name _____

4. Bicycle Checklist
Reread pages 283–286 of *A Trip to the Firehouse*, which tell how firefighters keep everything in perfect working order. Write a checklist.

- List these parts of a bicycle: *tires, handlebars, brakes, seat, pedals, chain, reflector, light,* and *bell or horn.* Look up any words you don't know in a dictionary.
- Think about what you need to do to keep a bicycle in good working order.
- Write a step on your checklist for each bicycle part.

Read your checklist to a classmate.

5. Helmet
Firefighters wear helmets. Who else wears helmets? Use a word web to answer this question. In the center circle, write the word *Helmets.* In the other circles, write other jobs or sports that use helmets. Share your web with a classmate.

6. Compounds
Play this game with a partner.

- Write each of the words on page 159 of the Practice Book on a separate index card. Then write each of these words on a separate index card: *up, side, house, stairs, in,* and *fire.*
- Lay all the cards face down on a desk. Player 1 turns over two cards. If the words make a compound word, player 1 gets to keep the cards. If not, it is player 2's turn.

DAY 1

1. Pretend Pets 30 MIN.   INDIVIDUAL
You might have children look through books about animals to help them choose their pretend pet.

2. Firefighter Interview 30 MIN.   PAIR
Remind children to ask *Who? What? Where? When? Why?* and *How?* questions. Ask volunteers to act out interviews for the class.

Additional Activities
- Audio Tape, *A Trip to the Firehouse*
- Practice Book p. 243, Spelling
- Technology: See p. 30.

DAY 2

3. *Catching Bailey* (Easy Theme Paperback) / *Harry's Pony* (On-Level Theme Paperback) 40 MIN.   INDIVIDUAL / PAIR
Materials: Graphic Organizer Master 3

If necessary, review story maps with children.

4. Bicycle Checklist 40 MIN.   INDIVIDUAL / PAIR
Remind children how firefighters maintained the fire truck in the selection. Have children use an encyclopedia.

English Language Learners Pair them with children who are more fluent in English.

Additional Activities
- Practice Book p. 163, Comprehension
- Practice Book p. 167, Spelling
- Practice Book p. 171, Grammar
- Technology: See p. 30.

DAY 3

5. Helmet 20 MIN.   INDIVIDUAL
Materials: Graphic Organizer Master 1

Ask children to describe a helmet they wear for a sport or other activity.

English Language Learners Have children work with a fluent English speaker.

6. Compounds 30 MIN. INDIVIDUAL / PAIR

Materials: index cards

Have children add other compound words to the game as they read the rest of the theme.

English Language Learners Have children work in pairs.

Additional Activities
- Practice Book, p. 168, Spelling
- Technology: See p. 30.

DAY 4

7. Uniforms 30 MIN. INDIVIDUAL / PAIR

Materials: drawing paper, crayons, and markers

Explain *uniform*. Ask children to describe special items of clothing they wear to school. (Social Studies)

English Language Learners Have on hand pictures of different workers wearing their uniforms.

8. Dial a Number 30 MIN. PAIR

Materials: photocopies of Transparency 3-12 and index cards

Discuss why phone numbers such as 911 are only for emergencies.

Additional Activities
- Practice Book p. 169, Spelling
- Practice Book p. 172, Grammar
- Technology: See p. 30.

DAY 5

9. Firehouse Noises 30 MIN. INDIVIDUAL / PAIR

Tell children that they will find clues to sounds in the storybook.

English Language Learners Have children work in pairs.

10. Fire Trucks 30 MIN. PAIR

Materials: drawing paper, crayons, and markers

Ask volunteers to share their poster with the class.

Additional Activities
- Anthology p. 290, Responding
- Practice Book p. 173, Grammar
- TE p. R9, R11, R23, R31, R40, R42
- Technology: See p. 30.

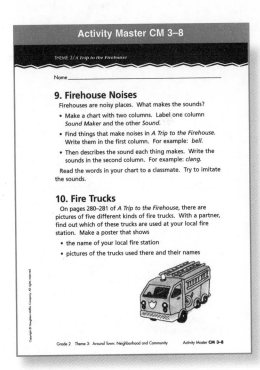

Activity Master CM 3–7

THEME 3/*A Trip to the Firehouse*

Name _____

7. Uniforms
Like firefighters, other people wear uniforms at work. For example: *crossing guard, police officer, nurse, mail carrier,* or *pilot.* Choose your favorite uniform.
- Draw a picture of a person wearing the uniform.
- Write about the person's job.

Show your picture to a classmate. Read the job description. Tell why the job is important.

8. Dial a Number
If you need help from people in your community, such as firefighters, you can call them with a telephone. With a classmate, make a telephone keypad.
- Use a large index card or cut a big rectangle from stiff paper.
- Divide the rectangle into 12 squares, like a telephone keypad.
- Then write in the numbers and symbols.
- One person reads phone numbers from the list of important numbers in Rosewood City.
- The other person dials the numbers on the keypad. Switch roles and dial again.

CM 3–7 Activity Master   Grade 2   Theme 3: Around Town: Neighborhood and Community

Activity Master CM 3–8

THEME 3/*A Trip to the Firehouse*

Name _____

9. Firehouse Noises
Firehouses are noisy places. What makes the sounds?
- Make a chart with two columns. Label one column *Sound Maker* and the other *Sound.*
- Find things that make noises in *A Trip to the Firehouse.* Write them in the first column. For example: *bell.*
- Then describes the sound each thing makes. Write the sounds in the second column. For example: *clang.*

Read the words in your chart to a classmate. Try to imitate the sounds.

10. Fire Trucks
On pages 280–281 of *A Trip to the Firehouse*, there are pictures of five different kinds of fire trucks. With a partner, find out which of these trucks are used at your local fire station. Make a poster that shows
- the name of your local fire station
- pictures of the trucks used there and their names

Grade 2   Theme 3: Around Town: Neighborhood and Community   Activity Master **CM 3–8**

THEME 3/SELECTION 3: *Big Bushy Mustache*

Assignments for Independent Activities

Assign for On-Level Students

Masters: CM 3-9—CM 3-12

Teacher support: GO-1, GO-3

Classroom materials: See list of materials with each activity.

Note: Many activities are appropriate for Extra Support students and English Language Learners.

Assign for Challenge Students

Masters: CH 3-5, CH 3-6

Teacher support: GO-1, GO-5

Classroom materials: Encyclopedia, poster boars, crayons, markers, paint, construction paper, glue, drawing paper

Note: Many activities are appropriate for advanced English Language Learners.

Check that students have read the selection or leveled reading specified for an activity.

- Anthology, pp. 298–335: *Big Bushy Mustache;* "Family Poems"
- Phonics Library: *Mouse's Crowded House; Hooray for Main Street*

- Theme Paperbacks: *Catching Bailey* (On My Way Practice Reader); *Harry's Pony* (On Level); *Solo Girl* (Challenge)

Provide copies of activity masters, graphic organizer masters, and challenge masters, as needed.

Additional Activities and Program Resources

Additional independent activities for this selection:

- Practice Book, pp. 177, 181, 184, 185, 186, 187, 189, 190, 191, 243
- Teacher's Resources Blackline Masters, Theme 3 Reading Cards 8, 9, 10
- TE pp. R13, R15, R25, R33, R41, R43
- TE Challenge pp. 328, 335, 335H, 344, R13, R15, R25, R33, R40, R42

Other program resources:

- Suggested in activities for this selection: Houghton Mifflin Social Studies Bookshelf: *City Green*
- Students' self-selected independent reading materials
- Students' journals or other independent writing materials

Get Set to Read *Big Bushy Mustache*

Education Place: www.eduplace.com for more activities related to *Big Bushy Mustache*

Accelerated Reader®, *Big Bushy Mustache*

Audiotape, *Big Bushy Mustache*

Extra Support lessons for *Big Bushy Mustache*

English language development lessons for *Big Bushy Mustache*

DAY 1

Preteach Phonics: Vowel Pairs *ow, ou*

Preteach Suffix *-ly*

Preview *Mouse's Crowded House*

• ES Handbook pp. 98–99 and masters PMES 3–5, TMES 3–5

Preteach Places and Jobs

Preteach Teacher Read Aloud *Cat Up a Tree*

Preteach Phonics: Vowel Pairs *ow, ou*

• ELL Handbook pp.102–103 and master ELL 3–7

DAY 2

Preteach Problem Solving

Preview Selection, Segment 1

• ES Handbook pp. 100–101 and masters PMES 3–6, TMES 3–6

Preteach School Workers

Preteach Get Set to Read; Anthology Selection

Reteach High-Frequency Words: *story*

• ELL Handbook pp. 104–105

DAY 3

Reteach High-Frequency Words

Reteach One and More Than One

Preview Selection, Segment 2

• ES Handbook pp. 102–103

Preteach Meals at Home and School

Reteach Phonics Review: Vowel Pairs *ai, ay*; High-Frequency Words: *behind, soldier*

• ELL Handbook pp. 106–107

DAY 4

Reteach Phonics: Vowel Pairs *ow, ou*

Preteach Suffixes *-ly, -ful*

Preview *Hooray for Main Street*

• ES Handbook pp. 104–105

Preteach Times of Day

Reteach Selection Summary and Review

Reteach Vocabulary: Using Context

• ELL Handbook pp. 108–109 and master ELL 3–8

DAY 5

Reteach Problem Solving

Revisit Selection, *Mouse's Crowded House*, and *Hooray for Main Street*

• ES Handbook pp. 106–107

Preteach Words of Greeting

Reteach Grammar: One and More Than One; Writing: Using Exact Nouns

• ELL Handbook pp. 110–111

Activities

DAY 1

1. Picture Search 30 MIN. INDIVIDUAL / PAIR

You may want to provide a photocopy of the cover. Children can circle all the differences on the picture. They can focus on color by looking at the original cover.

2. Who Am I? 30 MIN. INDIVIDUAL / PAIR

Materials: construction paper, markers, crayons, glue, scissors, and paint

Brainstorm with children lists of people they could be: a *king*, a *queen*, a *clown*, or a *pirate*. Ask children to share their costumes with the class. Remind them that they want to create a familiar costume so that classmates can guess who they are pretending to be.

> ### Additional Activities
>
> - Audio Tape, *Big Bushy Mustache*
> - Practice Book, p. 177, Phonics
> - Practice Book, p. 243, Spelling
> - Technology: See p. 34.

DAY 2

3. What If? 30 MIN. INDIVIDUAL

Ask volunteers to share their solutions with the class.

English Language Learners Have children work in pairs.

4. Spanish Glossary 40 MIN. INDIVIDUAL / PAIR

Materials: Spanish-English dictionary

If necessary, review glossary with children. You might want to combine entries to create a class glossary.

> ### Additional Activities
>
> - Practice Book, p. 181, Comprehension
> - Practice Book, p. 185, Spelling
> - Practice Book, p. 189, Grammar
> - Technology: See p. 34.

DAY 3

5. What Would He Say? 30 MIN. INDIVIDUAL / PAIR

Have children act out their dialogues for the class.

6. Ricky's Answers 30 MIN. INDIVIDUAL / PAIR

Instruct children to either write dialogue or describe a body language response, depending on the situation in the story.

Activity Master CM 3–9

THEME 3/*Big Bushy Mustache*

Name_____

1. Picture Search
Look carefully at the picture on the cover of *Big Bushy Mustache*. What is different about Ricky and his father?

- Examine colors, shapes, faces, clothes, and other features.
- Write at least seven things that are different.

Compare your list with a classmate's. Did your classmate see other things that are different? Talk about how Ricky and his father are different.

2. Who Am I?
If you could be someone else, who would you be? Make your own costume.

- Look at "Costumes and Disguises" on pages 296–297.
- Think about the different costumes you can make.
- Use construction paper and decorate your own costume.

Show your costume to a classmate. Have him or her guess who you are pretending to be and then tell why you chose your costume.

3. What If?
What if Ricky's dad didn't have a mustache to give him? What could Ricky do to solve his problem? Read pages 318–319 of *Big Bushy Mustache*. Make a list of the things that Ricky tried. Can you come up with different solutions? Write them down.

CM 3–9 Activity Master   Grade 2   Theme 3: Around Town: Neighborhood and Community

---

Activity Master CM 3–10

THEME 3/*Big Bushy Mustache*

Name_____

4. Spanish Glossary
Make a glossary of the Spanish words in *Big Bushy Mustache*.

- Find and list all the Spanish words in *Big Bushy Mustache*.
- Write a definition for each word on your list. Use a Spanish-English dictionary to help you.

Compare your glossary to a classmate's. Did you come up with the same definitions?

5. What Would He Say?
What do you think Ricky would say to his friends about where he got his new mustache? Write a dialogue between Ricky and one of his friends. Tell how Ricky lost his mustache and how his father helped him. Have the friend respond and ask questions about his story. Use the dialogue in the selection as a model. Be sure to use quotation marks before and after spoken words. Act out your dialogue with a classmate.

6. Ricky's Answers
Ricky meets three people on the street. Look at pages 308–309 of the story to find out about them.

- Think about what each person says or does. Should Ricky answer them in words, actions, or both?
- Write Ricky's response to these people.

Act out your responses with a classmate.

Grade 2   Theme 3: Around Town: Neighborhood and Community   Activity Master **CM 3–10**

English Language Learners Explain that they are going to write their own ideas. Have them work in pairs.

Additional Activities

- Practice Book, p. 186, Spelling
- Technology: See p. 34.

DAY 4

7. Language Survey   30 MIN.   INDIVIDUAL / SMALL GROUP

Have children check the spelling of any unfamiliar languages in a dictionary.

8. ¡Gracias, papá!   30 MIN.   INDIVIDUAL

Materials: *construction paper, crayons, markers, and glue*

Display cards on a classroom bulletin board.

Additional Activities

- Practice Book, p. 184, Phonics
- Practice Book, p. 187, Spelling
- Practice Book, p. 190, Grammar
- Technology: See p. 34.

DAY 5

9. Meaning Match   30 MIN.   INDIVIDUAL / PAIR

Materials: *index cards*

Extend the activity by having children add words from other stories to their game.

10. Calendar Quiz   30 MIN.   PAIR

Materials: *a calendar of the current year with holidays listed*

If necessary, review how to read a calendar with children.

Additional Activities

- Anthology, pp. 330–331, Responding
- Practice Book, p. 191, Grammar
- TE p. R13, R15, R25, R33, R41, R43
- Technology: See p. 34.

Activity Master CM 3–11

THEME 3/ *Big Bushy Mustache*

Name _____

7. Language Survey
Find out how many languages your classmates speak. Conduct a survey.
- Make a chart with three columns like the one below.
- Ask classmates, *What languages do you speak?*
- Write the name of the language in the first column.
- Write the name of the person who speaks the language in the second column.
- Add up the names in the second column. Write the total number in the last column.

Share your results with the class.

Language	Speakers	Total

8. ¡Gracias, papá!
In the story, Ricky's father shaves off his mustache so that Ricky can use it in the play. Make a thank-you card that Ricky might have made for his father. Title your card *¡Gracias, papá!*, which is Spanish for *Thank you, Father!* Draw pictures and designs and write a short message.

Activity Master CM 3–12

THEME 3/ *Big Bushy Mustache*

Name _____

9. Meaning Match
Play this matching game with a classmate.
- Find a list of the words on pages 178–179 of the Practice Book.
- Write each word on an index card. Write each meaning on a separate index card.
- Lay all the meanings face-up on your desk. Put all the words in a card pile face down.
- Player 1 chooses a word from the card pile and tries to match the word to its meaning. If player 1 makes a match, he or she keeps the cards. If not, it is the next player's turn.
- Play continues until all cards have been matched.

10. Calendar Quiz
Work with a partner to answer the following questions. Use a year-long calendar to help you.
- Which month has the least number of days?
- What day of the week does your birthday fall on?
- What months do you go to school?

THEME 3/SELECTION 4: *Jamaica Louise James*

Assignments for Independent Activities

Assign for On-Level Students

Classroom Management Handbook

Masters: CM 3-13—CM 3-16

Teacher support: GO-1, GO-3

Classroom materials: Drawing paper, crayons, markers, index cards, encyclopedia and books on artists, dictionary

Note: Many activities are appropriate for Extra Support students and English Language Learners.

Assign for Challenge Students

Challenge Handbook

Masters: CH 3-7, CH 3-8

Teacher support: GO-1, GO-5

Classroom materials: Drawing paper, crayons, markers

Note: Many activities are appropriate for advanced English Language Learners.

Check that students have read the selection or leveled reading specified for an activity.

- Anthology, pp. 338-367: *Jamaica Louise James;* "Sidewalk Sticks"
- Phonics Library: *The Clean Team; Big Hound's Lunch*

- Theme Paperbacks: *Catching Bailey* (On My Way Practice Reader); *Harry's Pony* (On Level); *Solo Girl* (Challenge)

Provide copies of activity masters, graphic organizer masters, and challenge masters, as needed.

Additional Activities and Program Resources

Additional independent activities for this selection:

- Practice Book, pp. 196, 199, 202, 203, 204, 205, 207, 208, 209, 245
- Teacher's Resources Blackline Masters, Theme 3 Reading Cards 12, 13, 14
- TE pp. R17, R19, R27, R35, R41, R43
- TE Challenge pp. 362, 367, 367H, 369, R17, R19, R27, R34, R41

Other program resources:

- Suggested in activities for this selection: Houghton Mifflin Social Studies Bookshelf: *City Green*
- Students' self-selected independent reading materials
- Students' journals or other independent writing materials

Get Set to Read *Jamaica Louise James*

Education Place: www.eduplace.com for more activities related to *Jamaica Louise James*

Accelerated Reader®, *Jamaica Louise James*

Audiotape, *Jamaica Louise James*

Extra Support lessons for *Jamaica Louise James*

 English language development lessons for *Jamaica Louise James*

DAY 1

Preteach Phonics: Vowel Pairs *ee, ea*
Preteach *-ture* Ending in Two-Syllable Words
Preview *The Clean Team*
- ES Handbook pp. 108–109 and masters PMES 3-7, TMES 3-7

Preteach Teamwork
Preteach Teacher Read Aloud *Millie's Garden*
Preteach Phonics: Vowel Pairs *ee, ea*
- ELL Handbook pp. 112–113 and master ELL 3-10

DAY 2

Preteach Making Inferences
Preview Selection, Segment 1
- ES Handbook pp. 110–111 and masters PMES 3-8, TMES 3-8

Preteach Family Members
Preteach Get Set to Read; Anthology Selection
Reteach High-Frequency Words: *believe, lady*
- ELL Handbook pp. 114–115

DAY 3

Reteach High-Frequency Words
Reteach Nouns that Change Spelling in Plural
Preview Selection, Segment 2
- ES Handbook pp. 112 –113

Preteach Money
Reteach Phonics Review: Vowel Pairs *ou, ow*; High-Frequency Word: *whole*
- ELL Handbook pp. 116–117

DAY 4

Reteach Phonics: Vowel Pairs *ee, ea*
Reteach Common Syllables *-tion, -ture*
Preview *Big Hound's Lunch*
- ES Handbook pp. 114–115

Preteach Colors
Reteach Selection Summary and Review
Reteach Vocabulary/Dictionary: Guidewords
- ELL Handbook pp. 118–119 and ELL 3-11

DAY 5

Reteach Problem Solving
Revisit Selection, *The Clean Team*, and *Big Hound's Lunch*
- ES Handbook pp. 116–117

Reteach Clothes
Reteach Grammar: Nouns That Change Spelling in the Plural; Writing: Audience
- ELL Handbook pp. 120–121

Activities

DAY 1

1. My Detailed Day   30 MIN.   INDIVIDUAL
Ask volunteers to share their stories with the class.

2. Transportation   30 MIN.   INDIVIDUAL
Materials: drawing paper, crayons, and markers

Display drawings on a classroom bulletin board.

English Language Learners Brainstorm kinds of transportation with children.

Additional Activities
• Audio Tape, *Jamaica Louise James*
• Practice Book, p. 196, High Frequency Words
• Practice Book, p. 245, Spelling
• Technology: See p. 38.

DAY 2

3. Birthday Gift   30 MIN.   INDIVIDUAL
Materials: drawing paper, crayons, and markers

Ask volunteers to share paragraphs with the class.

4. Word Scramble   30 MIN.   INDIVIDUAL
Tell students who are solving the scrambles that they can use the list of words on page 197 of the Practice Book to help them.

Additional Activities
• Practice Book, p. 199, Comprehension
• Practice Book, p. 203, Spelling
• Practice Book, p. 207, Grammar
• Technology: See p. 38.

DAY 3

5. *Catching Bailey* (On My Way Practice Reader)
30 MIN.   INDIVIDUAL / PAIR
Materials: index cards

You might want to collect all the cards into a larger game.

English Language Learners Have them work in pairs or in a group with other ELL children.

6. Tell Me Why 30 MIN. INDIVIDUAL / PAIR

Let children ask you about things in the drawing that they cannot identify.

English Language Learners Have children work in pairs.

Additional Activities

- Practice Book, p. 204, Spelling
- Technology: See p. 38.

DAY 4

7. Famous Artists 40 MIN. INDIVIDUAL

Materials: encyclopedia and books on artists

Brainstorm a list of artists with children.

English Language Learners Tell children if they want to, they can choose an artist from their country of origin.

8. Subway Art 30 MIN. INDIVIDUAL

Ask volunteers to share their journal entries with the class.

Additional Activities

- Practice Book, p. 202, Phonics
- Practice Book, p. 205, Spelling
- Practice Book, p. 208, Grammar
- Technology: See p. 38.

DAY 5

9. Character Descriptions 30 MIN. INDIVIDUAL / PAIR

Materials: Graphic Organizer Master 1

If necessary, review webs with children.

English Language Learners Have children work in pairs.

10. Guide Me 30 MIN. INDIVIDUAL

Materials: dictionary

If necessary, review guide words with children.

Additional Activities

- Anthology, pp. 364–365, Responding
- Practice Book, p. 209, Grammar
- TE p. R17, R19, R27, R35, R41, R43
- Technology: See p. 38.

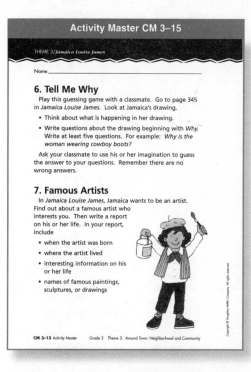

Activity Master CM 3–15

THEME 3/*Jamaica Louise James*

Name _____

6. Tell Me Why
Play this guessing game with a classmate. Go to page 345 in *Jamaica Louise James*. Look at Jamaica's drawing.
- Think about what is happening in her drawing.
- Write questions about the drawing beginning with *Why*. Write at least five questions. For example: *Why is the woman wearing cowboy boots?*

Ask your classmate to use his or her imagination to guess the answer to your questions. Remember there are no wrong answers.

7. Famous Artists
In *Jamaica Louise James*, Jamaica wants to be an artist. Find out about a famous artist who interests you. Then write a report on his or her life. In your report, include
- when the artist was born
- where the artist lived
- interesting information on his or her life
- names of famous paintings, sculptures, or drawings

CM 3–15 Activity Master   Grade 2   Theme 3: Around Town: Neighborhood and Community

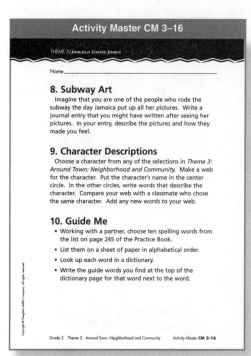

Activity Master CM 3–16

THEME 3/*Jamaica Louise James*

Name _____

8. Subway Art
Imagine that you are one of the people who rode the subway the day Jamaica put up all her pictures. Write a journal entry that you might have written after seeing her pictures. In your entry, describe the pictures and how they made you feel.

9. Character Descriptions
Choose a character from any of the selections in *Theme 3: Around Town: Neighborhood and Community*. Make a web for the character. Put the character's name in the center circle. In the other circles, write words that describe the character. Compare your web with a classmate who chose the same character. Add any new words to your web.

10. Guide Me
- Working with a partner, choose ten spelling words from the list on page 245 of the Practice Book.
- List them on a sheet of paper in alphabetical order.
- Look up each word in a dictionary.
- Write the guide words you find at the top of the dictionary page for that word next to the word.

Grade 2   Theme 3: Around Town: Neighborhood and Community   Activity Master **CM 3–16**

THEME 4/SELECTION 1: *Officer Buckle and Gloria*

Assignments for Independent Activities

Assign for On-Level Students

Masters: CM 4-1—CM 4-4

Teacher support: GO-2, GO-3, GO-5, GO-6, GO-7

Classroom materials: Crayons, markers, index cards, poster board

Note: Many activities are appropriate for Extra Support students and English Language Learners.

Check that students have read the selection or leveled reading specified for an activity.

- Anthology, pp. 18-55: *Officer Buckle and Gloria;* "The Story of Owney"
- Phonics Library: *A Park for Parkdale; Arthur's Book*

Assign for Challenge Students

Masters: CH 4-1, CH 4-2

Teacher support: GO-1, GO-3

Classroom materials: Poster board, crayons, scissors, glue, markers, construction paper

Note: Many activities are appropriate for advanced English Language Learners.

- Theme Paperbacks: *Sandy Goes to the Vet* (On My Way Practice Reader); *Raptors!* (On Level); *A Toad for Tuesday* (Challenge)

Provide copies of activity masters, graphic organizer masters, and challenge masters, as needed.

Additional Activities and Program Resources

Additional independent activities for this selection:

- Practice Book, pp. 3, 4, 8, 12, 13, 14, 16, 17
- Teacher's Resources Blackline Masters, Theme 4 Reading Cards 2, 3, 4
- TE pp. R5, R7, R15, R21, R29, R32
- TE Challenge pp. 11, 50, 55, 55H, R5, R7, R15, R21, R29

Other program resources:

- Suggested in activities for this selection: Houghton Mifflin Science DiscoveryWorks Trade Books: *How Big Were the Dinosaurs?*
- Students' self-selected independent reading materials
- Students' journals or other independent writing materials

Technology

Get Set to Read *Officer Buckle and Gloria*

Education Place: www.eduplace.com for more activities related to *Officer Buckle and Gloria*

Accelerated Reader®, *Officer Buckle and Gloria*

Audiotape, *Officer Buckle and Gloria*

Extra Support lessons for *Officer Buckle and Gloria*

 English language development lessons for *Officer Buckle and Gloria*

DAY 1

Preteach Phonics: Controlled Vowels *ar*
Preteach Phonics: Controlled Vowels *or, ore*
Preview *A Park for Parkdale*
• ES Handbook pp. 120–121 and masters PMES 4–1, TMES 4–1

Preteach Sounds Animals Make
Preteach Teacher Read Aloud *Oscar's Enormous Purr*
Preteach Phonics: *r*-controlled vowels *ar, or, ore*
• ELL Handbook pp. 124–125 and master ELL 4–1

DAY 2

Preteach Comprehension: Drawing Conclusions
Preview Selection, Segment 1
• ES Handbook pp. 122–123 and masters PMES 4–2, TMES 4–2

Preteach Words About Safety
Preteach Get Set to Read; Anthology Selection
Reteach High-Frequency Words: *board*
• ELL Handbook pp. 126–127

DAY 3

Reteach High-Frequency Words
Reteach Grammar: Words for Nouns (Pronouns)
Preview Selection, Segment 2
• ES Handbook pp. 124–125

Preteach Desserts
Reteach Phonics Review: The *-tion, -ture* Endings in Two-Syllable Words
Reteach High-Frequency Words: *listen, told*
• ELL Handbook pp. 128–129

DAY 4

Reteach Phonics: Controlled Vowels *ar*
Reteach Phonics: Controlled Vowels *or, ore*
Preview *Arthur's Book*
• ES Handbook pp. 126–127

Preteach Audience Behavior
Reteach Selection Summary and Review
Reteach Vocabulary/Dictionary: Entry Words
• ELL Handbook pp. 130–131 and master ELL 4–2

DAY 5

Reteach Comprehension: Drawing Conclusions
Revisit Selection, *A Park for Parkdale*, and *Arthur's Book*
• ES Handbook pp. 128–129

Preteach Shapes
Reteach Grammar: Words for Nouns
Reteach Writing: Writing Times
• ELL Handbook pp. 132–133

SELECTION 1:
Officer Buckle and Gloria

DAY 1

1. You're Invited   30 MIN.   INDIVIDUAL / PAIR
Materials: crayons and markers

Review how to write dates and time, if necessary. You might want to display invitations on a classroom bulletin board.

English Language Learners Review what an invitation is with children. Have them work in pairs.

2. Oscar's Events   30 MIN.   INDIVIDUAL / PAIR
Materials: index cards

Brainstorm with children some of the events from *Oscar's Enormous Purr.*

Additional Activities
• Audio Tape, *Officer Buckle and Gloria*
• Practice Book, pp. 3, 4, Phonics
• Practice Book, p. 229, Spelling
• Technology: See p. 42.

DAY 2

3. Crossing the Road   30 MIN.   INDIVIDUAL
Materials: poster board, crayons, and markers

Talk with children about the different traffic signs and lights on a street. Ask volunteers to act out how they cross a road safely. Display posters on a classroom bulletin board. (Social Studies)

4. Good Dog   30 MIN.   INDIVIDUAL
Remind children that they are using sentences that *tell*, and should start them with an action word.

English Language Learners Pair beginners with more advanced children.

Additional Activities
• Practice Book, p. 8, Comprehension
• Practice Book, p. 12, Spelling
• Practice Book, p. 16, Grammar
• Technology: See p. 42.

DAY 3

5. Missing Words   30 MIN.   INDIVIDUAL / PAIR
Tell children to look through the selection for safety tips.

6. Noise Words 30 MIN. INDIVIDUAL / PAIR

You might want to brainstorm with children different sound words.

English Language Learners Have children work in pairs.

> ### Additional Activities
> - Practice Book, p. 13, Spelling
> - Technology: See p. 42.

DAY 4

7. News Hound 40 MIN. INDIVIDUAL / PAIR

Remind children to be brief in their news report. Ask volunteers to read their stories to the class.

English Language Learners Have them work in pairs or a small group. You might want to review *Who? What? When? Where? How?* and *Why?* with children.

8. What's Next? 20 MIN. PAIR

If necessary, review predicting outcomes with children. Remind children to reread the story to find details to support their predictions.

> ### Additional Activities
> - Practice Book, p. 14, Spelling
> - Practice Book, p. 17, Grammar
> - Technology: See p. 42.

DAY 5

9. Guess Who? 30 MIN. INDIVIDUAL / PAIR

You might want to brainstorm with children lists of characters from the story and their corresponding pronouns.

10. Animal Match 30 MIN. INDIVIDUAL / PAIR

Materials: index cards

Tell children that sometimes baby animals have the same name as their parents. They can still use these animals in their game.

> ### Additional Activities
> - Anthology, pp. 52–53, Responding
> - Practice Book, p. 18, Grammar
> - TE p. R5, R7, R15, R21, R29, R32
> - Technology: See p. 42.

Activity Master CM 4–3

THEME 4/*Officer Buckle and Gloria*

Name_____

6. Noise Words
Look at page 46 in *Officer Buckle and Gloria*. There are four words that sound like a noise: *splat, splatter, sploosh,* and *smack.*
- Think of four more words that sound like a noise.
- Use each of your noise words in a sentence.
- Share your sentences with a classmate.

7. News Hound
Sometimes a reporter is called a *news hound.* This is because he or she "sniffs" out a story. Imagine you are a news hound. Write a short news story about what happened on page 46 and 47 of *Officer Buckle and Gloria.*
- Make notes of all the details from the pictures.
- Think of *Who? What? Where? When? How?* and *Why?* when you write.
- Make your story as descriptive as possible.
- Practice reading your news story.

8. What's Next?
Can you predict the outcome of *Officer Buckle and Gloria?* Do you think they will stay partners or break up? Support your prediction with details from the story.

CM 4–3 Activity Master   Grade 2 Theme 4: Amazing Animals

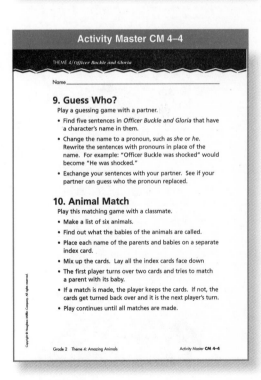

Activity Master CM 4–4

THEME 4/*Officer Buckle and Gloria*

Name_____

9. Guess Who?
Play a guessing game with a partner.
- Find five sentences in *Officer Buckle and Gloria* that have a character's name in them.
- Change the name to a pronoun, such as *she* or *he.* Rewrite the sentences with pronouns in place of the name. For example: "Officer Buckle was shocked" would become "He was shocked."
- Exchange your sentences with your partner. See if your partner can guess who the pronoun replaced.

10. Animal Match
Play this matching game with a classmate.
- Make a list of six animals.
- Find out what the babies of the animals are called.
- Place each name of the parents and babies on a separate index card.
- Mix up the cards. Lay all the index cards face down.
- The first player turns over two cards and tries to match a parent with its baby.
- If a match is made, the player keeps the cards. If not, the cards get turned back over and it is the next player's turn.
- Play continues until all matches are made.

Grade 2 Theme 4: Amazing Animals   Activity Master **CM 4–4**

THEME 4/SELECTION 2: *Ant*

Assignments for Independent Activities

Assign for On-Level Students

Masters: CM 4-5—CM 4-8
Teacher support: GO-2, GO-3, GO-5, GO-6, GO-7
Classroom materials: See list of materials with each activity.

Note: Many activities are appropriate for Extra Support students and English Language Learners.

Check that students have read the selection or leveled reading specified for an activity.

- Anthology, pp. 60–87: *Ant;* "The Ants Go Marching"
- Phonics Library: *Hank's Pandas; Marta's Larks*

Assign for Challenge Students

Masters: CH 4-3, CH 4-4
Teacher support: GO-1, GO-3
Classroom materials: Large drawing paper, tape, markers, encyclopedia, books about insects, drawing paper, dictionary, encyclopedia

Note: Many activities are appropriate for advanced English Language Learners.

- Theme Paperbacks: *Sandy Goes to the Vet* (On My Way Practice Reader); *Raptors!* (On Level); *A Toad for Tuesday* (Challenge)

Provide copies of activity masters, graphic organizer masters, and challenge masters, as needed.

Additional Activities and Program Resources

Additional independent activities for this selection:

- Practice Book, pp. 27, 31, 35, 36, 37, 39, 40, 41, 231
- Teacher's Resources Blackline Masters, Theme 4 Reading Cards 6, 7, 8
- TE pp. R9, R11, R17, R23, R30, R32
- TE Challenge pp. 82, 87H, R9, R11, R17, R23, R30

Other program resources:

- Suggested in activities for this selection: Houghton Mifflin Science DiscoveryWorks Trade Books: *How Big Were the Dinosaurs?*
- Students' self-selected independent reading materials
- Students' journals or other independent writing materials

Get Set to Read *Ant*

Education Place: www.eduplace.com for more activities related to *Ant*

Accelerated Reader®, *Ant*

Audiotape, *Ant*

Extra Support lessons for *Ant*

English language development lessons for *Ant*

DAY 1

Preteach Phonics: Final Consonant Clusters *nd, nk, nt*

Preteach Structural Analysis: Base Words and Endings: *-es, -ies* (Nouns)

Preview *Hank's Pandas*

• ES Handbook pp. 130–131 and masters PMES 4-3, TMES 4-3

Preteach Words That Mean *Amazing*

Preteach Teacher Read Aloud *An Octopus Is Amazing*

Preteach Structural Analysis: Base Words and Endings *-s, -es, -ies* (Nouns)

• ELL Handbook pp. 134–135 and master ELL 4-4

DAY 2

Preteach Comprehension: Text Organization

Preview Selection, Segment 1

• ES Handbook pp. 132–133 and masters PMES 4-4, TMES 4-4

Preteach Words About Ants

Preteach Get Set to Read; Anthology Selection

Reteach High-Frequency Word: *between*

• ELL Handbook pp. 136–137

DAY 3

Reteach High-Frequency Words

Reteach Grammar: Singular Possessive Nouns

Preview Selection, Segment 2

• ES Handbook pp. 134–135

Preteach Animal Groups

Reteach Phonics Review: *r*-controlled vowels *ar, or, ore*

Reteach High-Frequency Words: *care, weigh*

• ELL Handbook pp. 138–139

DAY 4

Reteach Phonics with *nd, nt, mp, ng, nk*

Reteach Structural Analysis: Base Words and Endings *-s, -es, -ies* (Nouns)

Preview *Marta's Larks*

• ES Handbook pp. 136–137

Preteach Continents

Reteach Selection Summary and Review

Reteach Vocabulary: Using a Thesaurus

• ELL Handbook pp. 140–141 and master ELL 4-5

DAY 5

Reteach Comprehension Text Organization

Revisit Selection, *Hank's Pandas*, and *Marta's Larks*

• ES Handbook pp. 138–139

Preteach Numbers and Numerals

Reteach Grammar: Singular Possessive Nouns

Reteach Writing: Using *I* and *me*

• ELL Handbook pp. 142–143

Activities

Activity Master CM 4–5

THEME 4/*Ant*

Name_____

1. Cooperation

Ants cooperate. *Cooperation* means working together. Divide a sheet of paper into two columns.

- In the first column, write five ways that ants cooperate in the story *Ant*.
- Compare the five ways to how people cooperate. Write your ideas in the second column. For example: *Ants feed their babies and each other. People feed their babies.*

Share your chart with a classmate.

2. Giant Pandas

In the story *Hank's Pandas*, Hank works with giant pandas at a zoo. The National Zoo in Washington, D.C. has two giant pandas that were given to the United States by China. Find out about these pandas in an encyclopedia or on the Internet. Write a paragraph about what you learn. Draw a picture to go with your paragraph.

3. Ant Picnic

The ants from the story *Ant* are having a picnic.

- Find each kind of ants' favorite food in *Ant*.
- Make a picnic announcement. Write the menu on it. Be sure to include at least one food for each kind of ant.
- Decorate the announcement.

CM 4–5 Activity Master   Grade 2 Theme 4: Amazing Animals

Activity Master CM 4–6

THEME 4/*Ant*

Name_____

4. Match the Ants

Create a matching game. You need index cards.

- Make a list of all the kinds of ants in the story *Ant*.
- Write two details about each kind of ant next to its name.
- Write the name of each ant on one index card and its two details on another.
- Lay all the cards face down on your desk.
- The first player turns over two cards, trying to match the ant with its details. If they match, the player keeps the match. If not, the player turns the cards over and it is the next player's turn.

5. Insect Poetry

Write a counting poem about insects.

- Each line of the poem must begin with a number and the name of an insect. For example: *Three flies sat on a tree.* Try to use a different insect for each line.
- Start the poem with number one and continue to number ten.
- Draw a picture to go with your poem.
- Read your poem to a classmate.

Grade 2 Theme 4: Amazing Animals   Activity Master **CM 4–6**

DAY 1

1. Cooperation   30 MIN.   INDIVIDUAL / PAIR

You might want to create a class chart of ways both ants and people cooperate. (Science)

English Language Learners You might want to review the term cooperation with students and brainstorm examples of people cooperating.

2. Giant Pandas   40 MIN.   INDIVIDUAL

Materials: encyclopedia and Internet access

Refer children to http://pandas.si.edu/mei_tian/index.htm for information on the great pandas at the National Zoo. (Science)

Additional Activities

- Audio Tape, *Ant*
- Practice Book, p. 27, Phonics
- Practice Book, p. 231, Spelling
- Technology: See p. 46.

DAY 2

3. Ant Picnic   30 MIN.   INDIVIDUAL

Materials: drawing paper, construction paper, crayons, and markers

Explain to children that their announcement should have a title, picnic menu, and notes about where and when. (Social Studies) (Science)

4. Match the Ants   30 MIN.   INDIVIDUAL / PAIR

Materials: index cards

Have children expand the game to include other insects.

Additional Activities

- Practice Book, p. 31, Comprehension
- Practice Book, p. 35, Spelling
- Practice Book, p. 39, Grammar
- Technology: See p. 46.

DAY 3

5. Insect Poetry   30 MIN.   INDIVIDUAL / PAIR

Materials: encyclopedias and other science books on insects, drawing paper, crayons, and markers

Tell children to refer to encyclopedias and other reference sources.

English Language Learners Have children work in pairs.

6. Ant Maze 30 MIN. INDIVIDUAL / PAIR

Materials: *drawing paper and examples of mazes*

Remind children to use examples as a model. Tell them to think about the path of an ant when drawing their mazes.

Additional Activities
- Practice Book, p. 36, Spelling
- Technology: See p. 46.

DAY 4

7. Fun Fact Poster 30 MIN. INDIVIDUAL

Materials: *poster board, crayons, and markers*

You might want to display posters on a classroom bulletin board. (Science)

8. Human Antennae 30 MIN. INDIVIDUAL

Materials: *small classroom objects and a bag or small container with a lid*

Make sure bags and containers are not transparent. Talk with children about how antennae are like human hands. (Science)

Additional Activities
- Practice Book, p. 37, Spelling
- Practice Book, p. 40, Grammar
- Technology: See p. 46.

DAY 5

9. *Raptors* (On-Level Theme Paperback) 40 MIN. INDIVIDUAL / PAIR
Materials: *Graphic Organizer Master 10*

Instruct children to stop reading at different intervals in the book and fill in the chart.

10. *Sandy Goes to the Vet* (On My Way Practice Reader)
  30 MIN. INDIVIDUAL / PAIR

Materials: *Graphic Organizer Master 3*

Ask volunteers to retell the story for the class.

Additional Activities
- Anthology, pp. 84–85, Responding
- Practice Book, p. 41, Grammar
- TE p. R9, R11, R17, R23, R30, R32
- Technology: See p. 46.

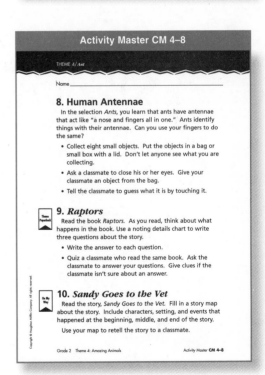

Activity Master CM 4–7

THEME 4/*Ant*

Name _____

6. Ant Maze
Draw an ant maze on a piece of drawing paper. Use examples of mazes to help you.
- Draw a line at the top of the page to show the ground level. Leave an opening. Label it *Enter*.
- Draw a path from the opening to the bottom right corner of the paper. Label this *Home*.
- Make lots of twists and turns in your main path.
- Add sections off the main path that lead to dead ends.

Ask a classmate to solve the maze.

7. Fun Fact Poster
Choose one of the kinds of ants mentioned in *Ant*. Make a fun fact poster about that ant.
- Go to pages 58–59 in the story, *Ant*. You will see examples of fun facts.
- Find two fun facts about the ant you chose.
- Write the fun facts on your poster.
- Add drawings of the ant to your poster.

Share your poster with the class. Explain the fun facts.

Activity Master CM 4–8

THEME 4/*Ant*

Name _____

8. Human Antennae
In the selection *Ants*, you learn that ants have antennae that act like "a nose and fingers all in one." Ants identify things with their antennae. Can you use your fingers to do the same?
- Collect eight small objects. Put the objects in a bag or small box with a lid. Don't let anyone see what you are collecting.
- Ask a classmate to close his or her eyes. Give your classmate an object from the bag.
- Tell the classmate to guess what it is by touching it.

9. Raptors
Read the book *Raptors*. As you read, think about what happens in the book. Use a noting details chart to write three questions about the story.
- Write the answer to each question.
- Quiz a classmate who read the same book. Ask the classmate to answer your questions. Give clues if the classmate isn't sure about an answer.

10. *Sandy Goes to the Vet*
Read the story, *Sandy Goes to the Vet*. Fill in a story map about the story. Include characters, setting, and events that happened at the beginning, middle, and end of the story.
Use your map to retell the story to a classmate.

THEME 4/SELECTION 3: *The Great Ball Game*

Assignments for Independent Activities

Assign for On-Level Students

Classroom Management Handbook

Masters: CM 4-9—CM 4-12

Teacher support: GO-2, GO-3, GO-5, GO-6, GO-7

Classroom materials: See list of materials with each activity.

Note: Many activities are appropriate for Extra Support students and English Language Learners.

Check that students have read the selection or leveled reading specified for an activity.

- Anthology, pp. 90-115: *The Great Ball Game;* "Bat Attitude"
- Phonics Library: *Crow's Plan; Brent Skunk Sings*

Assign for Challenge Students

Challenge Handbook

Masters: CH 4-5, CH 4-6

Teacher support: GO-1, GO-3

Classroom materials: See list of materials with each activity.

Note: Many activities are appropriate for advanced English Language Learners.

- Theme Paperbacks: *Sandy Goes to the Vet* (On My Way Practice Reader); *Raptors!* (On Level); *A Toad for Tuesday* (Challenge)

Provide copies of activity masters, graphic organizer masters, and challenge masters, as needed.

Additional Activities and Program Resources

Additional independent activities for this selection:

- Practice Book, pp. 44, 48, 52, 53, 54, 56, 57, 58, 231
- Teacher's Resources Blackline Masters, Theme 4 Reading Cards 10, 11, 12
- TE pp. R13, R19, R25, R31, R33
- TE Challenge pp. 108, 115, 115H, 117, R13, R19, R25, R29, R31, R33

Other program resources:

- Suggested in activities for this selection: Houghton Mifflin Science DiscoveryWorks Trade Books: *How Big Were the Dinosaurs?*
- Students' self-selected independent reading materials
- Students' journals or other independent writing materials

Technology

Get Set to Read *The Great Ball Game*

Education Place: www.eduplace.com for more activities related to *The Great Ball Game*

Accelerated Reader®, *The Great Ball Game*

Audiotape, *The Great Ball Game*

Extra Support lessons for *The Great Ball Game*

English language development lessons for *The Great Ball Game*

DAY 1

Preteach Phonics: Vowel Pairs *oa, ow*
Preview *Crow's Plan*

- ES Handbook pp. 140–141 and masters PMES 4–5, TMES 4–5

Preteach Words That Compare
Preteach Teacher Read Aloud *The Little Fly and the Great Moose*
Preteach Phonics: Vowel Pairs *oa, ow*

- ELL Handbook pp. 144–145 and master ELL 4–7

DAY 2

Preteach Comprehension: Cause and Effect
Preview Selection, Segment 1

- ES Handbook pp. 142–143 and masters PMES 4–6, TMES 4–6

Preteach Words About Games
Preteach Get Set to Read; Anthology Selection
Reteach High-Frequency Words: *ago, field*

- ELL Handbook pp. 146–147

DAY 3

Reteach High-Frequency Words
Reteach Grammar: Plural to Possessive Nouns
Preview Selection, Segment 2

- ES Handbook pp. 144–145

Preteach Parts of a Bird
Reteach Phonics Review: Final Consonant Clusters *nd, nt, mp, ng, nk*
Reteach High-Frequency Words: *half, war*

- ELL Handbook pp. 148–149

DAY 4

Reteach Phonics: Vowel Pairs *oa, ow* (long *o*)
Preview *Brent Skunk Sings*

- ES Handbook pp. 146–147

Preteach Parts of an Animal
Reteach Selection Summary and Review
Reteach Vocabulary/Dictionary: Parts of a Dictionary Entry

- ELL Handbook pp. 150–151 and master ELL 4–8

DAY 5

Reteach Comprehension: Cause and Effect
Revisit Selection, *Crow's Plan*, and *Brent Skunk Sings*

- ES Handbook pp. 148–149

Reteach Cardinal Directions
Reteach Grammar: Plural Possessive Nouns
Reteach Writing: Adding Details

- ELL Handbook pp. 152–153

Activities

Activity Master CM 4–9

THEME 4/*The Great Ball Game*

Name _____

1. Teamwork

In *The Great Ball Game*, the members of each team contribute different skills to the game. Pick new animals to be on the "teeth" team and list their skills.

• Divide a sheet of paper in half. Label one half *column 1* and the other half *column 2*.

• In column 1, list six new animals for the "teeth" team.

• In column 2, write notes about each new team member's skill and why he or she is good for the team. For example: *A giraffe has a long neck and runs fast.*

• Draw your favorite new team member.

Read and explain your choices to a classmate.

 2. *Crow's Plan*

Reread the story *Crow's Plan*. What is the problem that the animals try to solve? How do they solve it? Use a problem/solution chart to show what happens in the story. Share your chart with a classmate.

3. Animal Homes

Choose an animal from *The Great Ball Game* and one other animal that interests you. Where do these animals live? Find out about each of the animal's homes in the encyclopedia or other books. Make notes about where it lives or builds its home. Then use a Venn diagram to compare and contrast the two animals' homes.

CM 4–9 Activity Master   Grade 2 Theme 4: Amazing Animals

Activity Master CM 4–10

THEME 4/*The Great Ball Game*

Name _____

4. Animal Charades

Play animal charades with some classmates.

• Make a word card for each animal in *The Great Ball Game*.

• Shuffle the cards and place them face down.

• Choose a card and look at the name. Keep it a secret.

• Act like the animal without using words. Ask your classmates to guess what animal you are.

• For each guess, say *yes* or *no*. Do not give hints.

Take turns playing until all the cards are played.

5. Story Dictionary

Make a list of five words from the story that a reader might need help with. Put the words in alphabetical order. Make a dictionary entry for each word. Be sure that

• each word has a meaning and a sample sentence

• if possible, each word has a picture

Use your glossary to remind you how to write a dictionary entry. Use a dictionary to help you with meanings. Do not pick words that are already in your glossary.

Grade 2 Theme 4: Amazing Animals   Activity Master **CM 4–10**

DAY 1

1. Teamwork   30 MIN.   INDIVIDUAL / PAIR

Materials: drawing paper, crayons, and markers

Tell children to think about an animal's natural abilities and physical characteristics before they include them on the team. (Science)

English Language Learners Have children work in pairs.

2. *Crow's Plan* (Phonics Library)   30 MIN.   INDIVIDUAL / PAIR

Materials: Graphic Organizer Master 6

If necessary, review problem and solution with children.

> **Additional Activities**
> • Audio Tape, *The Great Ball Game*
> • Practice Book, p. 44, Phonics
> • Practice Book, p. 231, Spelling
> • Technology: See p. 50.

DAY 2

3. Animal Homes   30 MIN.   INDIVIDUAL

Materials: Graphic Organizer Master 2, encyclopedia, and books on animals

Remind children they are looking for *similarities* and *differences* in their homes. (Science)

English Language Learners Brainstorm with children lists of animals not in the selection.

4. Animal Charades   30 MIN.   SMALL GROUP

Materials: index cards

Have children expand the game by adding animals not in the selection.

> **Additional Activities**
> • Practice Book, p. 48, Comprehension
> • Practice Book, p. 52, Spelling
> • Practice Book, p. 56, Grammar
> • Technology: See p. 50.

DAY 3

5. Story Dictionary   30 MIN.   INDIVIDUAL

Materials: dictionary

Display children's entries on a classroom bulletin board.

English Language Learners Pair beginners with more advanced children.

6. Name That Team! <u>30 MIN.</u> INDIVIDUAL

Materials: drawing paper, construction paper, crayons, and markers

Brainstorm with children the names of some sports teams and have them describe their emblems, logos, or badges.

> ### Additional Activities
> • Practice Book, p. 53, Spelling   • Technology: See p. 50.

DAY 4

7. Animal Fables <u>40 MIN.</u> INDIVIDUAL / PAIR

Materials: copies of Aesop's Fables *or other animal fables*

Tell children that sometimes fables explain things and teach lessons.

8. Artist <u>40 MIN.</u> INDIVIDUAL / PAIR

Materials: construction paper, wallpaper scraps, buttons, thread, string, cotton balls, felt, and other textured materials, crayons, paint, and markers.

Tell children to overlap the materials. (Art)

> ### Additional Activities
> • Practice Book, p. 54, Spelling   • Technology: See p. 50.
> • Practice Book, p. 57, Grammar

DAY 5

9. Sticky Situation <u>30 MIN.</u> INDIVIDUAL / PAIR

Brainstorm effects of the new event with them.

10. News Article <u>40 MIN.</u> INDIVIDUAL

Review writing a news article with children. Ask volunteers to read their articles to the class.

> ### Additional Activities
> • Anthology, pp. 110–111,   • TE p. R13, R19, R25, R31, R33
>   Responding   • Technology: See p. 50.
> • Practice Book, p. 58, Grammar

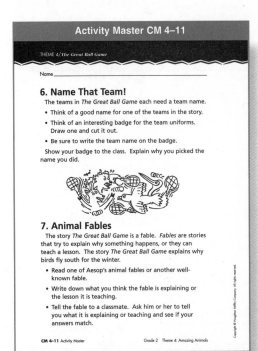

Activity Master CM 4–11

THEME 4/*The Great Ball Game*

Name _____

6. Name That Team!
The teams in *The Great Ball Game* each need a team name.
• Think of a good name for one of the teams in the story.
• Think of an interesting badge for the team uniforms. Draw one and cut it out.
• Be sure to write the team name on the badge.
Show your badge to the class. Explain why you picked the name you did.

7. Animal Fables
The story *The Great Ball Game* is a fable. *Fables* are stories that try to explain why something happens, or they can teach a lesson. The story *The Great Ball Game* explains why birds fly south for the winter.
• Read one of Aesop's animal fables or another well-known fable.
• Write down what you think the fable is explaining or the lesson it is teaching.
• Tell the fable to a classmate. Ask him or her to tell you what it is explaining or teaching and see if your answers match.

CM 4–11 Activity Master   Grade 2 Theme 4: Amazing Animals

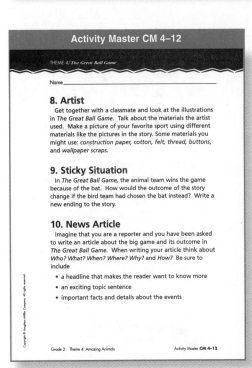

Activity Master CM 4–12

THEME 4/*The Great Ball Game*

Name _____

8. Artist
Get together with a classmate and look at the illustrations in *The Great Ball Game*. Talk about the materials the artist used. Make a picture of your favorite sport using different materials like the pictures in the story. Some materials you might use: *construction paper, cotton, felt, thread, buttons, and wallpaper scraps.*

9. Sticky Situation
In *The Great Ball Game*, the animal team wins the game because of the bat. How would the outcome of the story change if the bird team had chosen the bat instead? Write a new ending to the story.

10. News Article
Imagine that you are a reporter and you have been asked to write an article about the big game and its outcome in *The Great Ball Game*. When writing your article think about *Who? What? When? Where? Why?* and *How?* Be sure to include
• a headline that makes the reader want to know more
• an exciting topic sentence
• important facts and details about the events

Grade 2 Theme 4: Amazing Animals   Activity Master CM 4–12

THEME 5/SELECTION 1: *Brothers and Sisters*

Assignments for Independent Activities

Assign for On-Level Students

Masters: CM 5-1—CM 5-4

Teacher support: GO-1, GO-3, GO-8

Classroom materials: Graph paper, index cards, drawing paper, crayons, markers, art paper or construction paper, scissors

Note: Many activities are appropriate for Extra Support students and English Language Learners.

Assign for Challenge Students

Masters: CH 5-1, CH 5-2

Teacher support: GO-1, GO-4

Classroom materials: Construction paper, scissors, glue, ribbon

Note: Many activities are appropriate for advanced English Language Learners.

Check that students have read the selection or leveled reading specified for an activity.

- Anthology, pp. 126–151: *Brothers and Sisters;* "Brother and Sister Poems"
- Phonics Library: *My Sister Joan; The Big Party Plan*

- Theme Paperbacks: *Swim, Dad!* (On My Way Practice Reader); *Tonight is Carnival* (On Level); *Grandaddy and Janetta* (Challenge)

Provide copies of activity masters, graphic organizer masters, and challenge masters, as needed.

Additional Activities and Program Resources

Additional independent activities for this selection:

- Practice Book, pp. 69, 73, 77, 78, 79, 81, 82, 83, 234
- Teacher's Resources Blackline Masters, Theme 5 Reading Cards 2, 3, 4
- TE pp. R5, R19, R27, R38, R40
- TE Challenge pp. 119, 144, 151, 151H, 163, R5, R19, R27, R38

Other program resources:

- Suggested in activities for this selection: Houghton Mifflin Social Studies Bookshelf: *It Takes a Village; Dear Annie*
- Students' self-selected independent reading materials
- Students' journals or other independent writing materials

Get Set to Read *Brothers and Sisters*

Education Place: www.eduplace.com for more activities related to *Brothers and Sisters*

Accelerated Reader®, *Brothers and Sisters*

Audiotape, *Brothers and Sisters*

Extra Support lessons for *Brothers and Sisters*

English language development lessons for *Brothers and Sisters*

DAY 1

Preteach Phonics: The *-er* Ending in Two-Syllable Words

Preview *My Sister Joan*

- ES Handbook pp. 152–153 and masters PMES 5-1, TMES 5-1

Preteach Birthdays

Preteach Teacher Read Aloud *Only Emily*

Preteach Phonics: The *-er* Ending in Two-Syllable Words

- ELL Handbook pp. 156–157 and master ELL 5-1

DAY 2

Preteach Comprehension: Making Generalizations

Preview Selection, Segment 1

- ES Handbook pp. 154–155 and masters PMES 5-2, TMES 5-2

Preteach Family Members

Preteach Get Set to Read; Anthology Selection

Reteach High-Frequency Word: *middle*

- ELL Handbook pp. 158–159

DAY 3

Reteach High-Frequency Words

Reteach Grammar: Verbs

Preview Selection, Segment 2

- ES Handbook pp. 156–157

Preteach Games

Reteach Phonics Review: Vowel Pairs *oa, ow*

Reteach High-Frequency Words: *trouble, uncle*

- ELL Handbook pp. 160–161

DAY 4

Reteach The *-er* Ending in Two-Syllable Words

Preview *The Big Party Plan*

- ES Handbook pp. 158–159

Preteach Feelings

Reteach Selection Summary and Review

Reteach Vocabulary: Word Families

- ELL Handbook pp. 162–163 and master ELL 5-2

DAY 5

Reteach Making Generalizations

Revisit Selection, *The Big Party Plan*, and *My Sister Joan*

- ES Handbook pp. 160–161

Reteach Grades in School

Reteach Grammar: Verbs

Reteach Writing: Voice

- ELL Handbook pp. 164–165

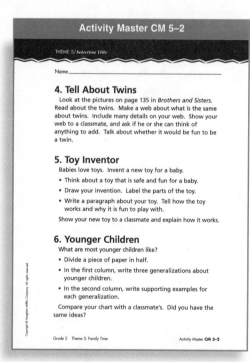

1. You're the Teacher 30 MIN. INDIVIDUAL / PAIR

Tell children they can think of things to teach a baby at any age. (Social Studies)

English Language Learners Have children work in pairs to discuss ideas about babies in their homes or babies that they know.

2. *My Sister Joan* (Phonics Library) 30 MIN. INDIVIDUAL / PAIR

Ask volunteers to share their paragraphs with the class.

English Language Learners Explain *nicknames* to children.

Additional Activities
- Audio Tape, *Brothers and Sisters*
- Practice Book, p. 69, Phonics
- Practice Book, p. 234, Spelling
- Technology: See p. 54.

3. Privacy Rules 30 MIN. INDIVIDUAL

Help children understand the term *privacy.* Instruct them to use imperative sentences, or commands, in their rules. (Social Studies)

4. Tell About Twins 30 MIN. INDIVIDUAL / PAIR
Materials: Graphic Organizer Master 1

If there is a child in class who is a twin, you may want to ask him or her to tell the class what it's like to be a twin. (Social Studies)

Additional Activities
- Practice Book, p. 73, Comprehension
- Practice Book, p. 77, Spelling
- Practice Book, p. 81, Grammar
- Technology: See p. 54.

5. Toy Inventor 40 MIN. INDIVIDUAL / PAIR / SMALL GROUP
Materials: graph paper

Display children's inventions on a classroom bulletin board. (Social Studies) (Science)

6. Younger Children 30 MIN. INDIVIDUAL

Ask volunteers to share their generalizations with the class. (Social Studies)

Additional Activities

• Practice Book, p. 78, Spelling   • Technology: See p. 54.

DAY 4

7. Brother, Sister Survey 30 MIN. INDIVIDUAL

You may want to do a follow-up activity around the results of the survey. (Social Studies) (Math)

8. Make the Connection 20 MIN. INDIVIDUAL / PAIR

Materials: *index cards, drawing paper, crayon, and markers*

Instruct children to write both male and female names on word cards. (Social Studies)

Additional Activities

• Practice Book, p. 79, Spelling   • Technology: See p. 54.
• Practice Book, p. 82, Grammar

DAY 5

9. Family Poetry 30 MIN. INDIVIDUAL

Materials: *drawing paper, crayons, and markers*

Display children's poems on a classroom bulletin board.

English Language Learners Have children work in pairs.

10. You're Special! 30 MIN. INDIVIDUAL

Materials: *art paper or construction paper, scissors, and markers*

Tell children they can choose to write poems in rhyme or plain verse. Remind them to use a dictionary to check spelling. (Social Studies)

Additional Activities

• Anthology, pp. 146–147,   • TE p. R5, R19, R27, R38, R40
  Responding   • Technology: See p. 54.
• Practice Book, p. 83, Grammar

THEME 5/SELECTION 2: *Jalapeño Bagels*

Assignments for Independent Activities

Assign for On-Level Students

Masters: CM 5-5—CM 5-8

Teacher support: GO-1, GO-3, GO-8

Classroom materials: Drawing paper, crayons, markers, encyclopedia, poster board, index cards, craft dough or clay

Note: Many activities are appropriate for Extra Support students and English Language Learners.

Assign for Challenge Students

Masters: CH 5-3, CH 5-4

Teacher support: GO-1, GO-4

Classroom materials: Encyclopedia, globe, poster board, index cards, crayons, markers

Note: Many activities are appropriate for advanced English Language Learners.

Check that students have read the selection or leveled reading specified for an activity.

- Anthology, pp. 156–181: *Jalapeño Bagels;* "Welcome to the Kitchen"

- Phonics Library: *Lost and Found; What Will Lester Be?*

- Theme Paperbacks: *Swim, Dad!* (On My Way Practice Reader); *Tonight is Carnival* (On Level); *Grandaddy and Janetta* (Challenge)

Provide copies of activity masters, graphic organizer masters, and challenge masters, as needed.

Additional Activities and Program Resources

Additional independent activities for this selection:

- Practice Book, pp. 91, 96, 99, 100, 101, 102, 104, 105, 106, 235

- Teacher's Resources Blackline Masters, Theme 5 Reading Cards 6, 7, 8

- TE pp. R7, R9, R21, R29, R38, R40

- TE Challenge pp. 176, 181H, R7, R9, R21, R29, R38

Other program resources:

- Suggested in activities for this selection: Houghton Mifflin Social Studies Bookshelf: *It Takes a Village; Dear Annie*

- Students' self-selected independent reading materials

- Students' journals or other independent writing materials

Get Set to Read *Jalapeño Bagels*

Education Place: www.eduplace.com for more activities related to *Jalapeño Bagels*

Accelerated Reader®, *Jalapeño Bagels*

Audiotape, *Jalapeño Bagels*

Extra Support lessons for *Jalapeño Bagels*

English language development lessons for *Jalapeño Bagels*

DAY 1

Preteach Structural Analysis: Contradictions
Preteach The *-le* Ending in Two-Syllable Words
Preview *Lost and Found*
• ES Handbook pp. 162–163 and masters PMES 5-3, TMES 5-3

Preteach Following Directions
Preteach Teacher Read Aloud *Jennifer and Granddad's Garden*
Preteach Structural Analysis: Contradictions
• ELL Handbook pp. 166–167 and master ELL 5-4

DAY 2

Preteach Following Directions
Preview Selection, Segment 1
• ES Handbook pp. 164–165 and masters PMES 5-4, TMES 5-4

Preteach Bakery Items
Preteach Get Set to Read; Anthology Selection
Reteach High-Frequency Word: *early*
• ELL Handbook pp. 168–169

DAY 3

Reteach High-Frequency Words
Reteach Grammar: Verbs That Tell About Now
Preview Selection, Segment 2
• ES Handbook pp. 166–167

Preteach Baking
Reteach Phonics Review: The *-er* Ending in Two-Syllable Words
Reteach High-Frequency Words: *hair, instead*
• ELL Handbook pp. 170–171

DAY 4

Reteach Phonics: Contractions
Reteach The *-le* Ending in Two-Syllable Words
Preview *What Will Lester Be?*
• ES Handbook pp. 168–169

Preteach Cooking Measurements
Reteach Selection Summary and Review
Reteach Vocabulary/Dictionary: Word Meanings
• ELL Handbook pp. 172–173 and master ELL 5-5

DAY 5

Reteach Following Directions
Revisit Selection, *Lost and Found*, and *What Will Lester Be?*
• ES Handbook pp. 170–171

Reteach Foods from Different Countries
Reteach Grammar: Verbs That Tell About Now
Reteach Writing: Keeping to the Point
• ELL Handbook pp. 174–175

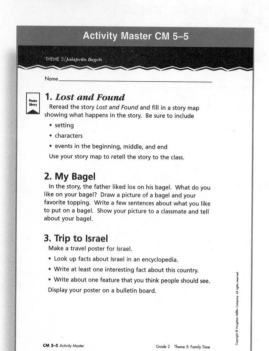

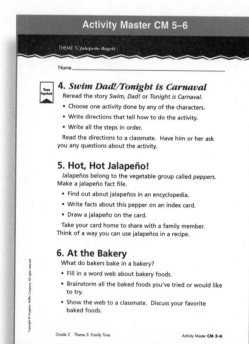

DAY 1

1. *Lost and Found* (Phonics Library) <u>30 MIN.</u> INDIVIDUAL
Materials: *Graphic Organizer Master 3*

If necessary, review story maps with children.

2. My Bagel <u>20 MIN.</u> INDIVIDUAL
Materials: *drawing paper, crayons, and markers*

Display drawings on a classroom bulletin board.

Additional Activities
- Audio Tape, *Jalapeño Bagels*
- Practice Book, p. 91, Phonics
- Practice Book, p. 235, Spelling
- Technology: See p. 58.

DAY 2

3. Trip to Israel <u>40 MIN.</u> INDIVIDUAL / PAIR
Materials: *encyclopedia and poster board*

Start the activity by showing Israel's location on a globe. Children may need connections for the words *Israeli, Jewish,* and *Yiddish.* (Social Studies)

4. *Swim Dad!* (Easy Theme Paperback) /*Tonight is Carnaval* (On-Level Theme Paperback) <u>40 MIN.</u> INDIVIDUAL / PAIR
Tell children to make notes as they read, since "how-to" directions may be scattered throughout the story. (Social Studies) (Science)

English Language Learners Before writing, have children pantomime or act out an activity.

Additional Activities
- Practice Book, p. 96, Comprehension
- Practice Book, p. 100, Spelling
- Practice Book, p. 104, Grammar
- Technology: See p. 58.

DAY 3

5. Hot, Hot Jalapeño! <u>20 MIN.</u> INDIVIDUAL / PAIR
Materials: *index cards and encyclopedia*

Ask children to include facts from *Jalapeño Bagels.* (Science)

6. At the Bakery 30 MIN. INDIVIDUAL / PAIR

Materials: *Graphic Organizer Master 1*

Tell children to look at pictures in the story if they need more ideas. (Social Studies)

> ### Additional Activities
> • Practice Book, p. 101, Spelling • Technology: See p. 58.

DAY 4

7. Dream Ice Cream 30 MIN. INDIVIDUAL

Materials: *index cards*

Review simple cooking measurements such as spoon and cup. Tell children that scoop is a measurement used for ice cream. (Science) (Math)

English Language Learners Provide measuring cups and spoons in both standard and metric measures for children to examine.

8. Favorite Flavor Survey 40 MIN. INDIVIDUAL / PAIR

Use Transparency 2-14 to review how to make a graph. (Math)

> ### Additional Activities
> • Practice Book, p. 99, Phonics • Practice Book, p. 105, Grammar
> • Practice Book, p. 102, Spelling • Technology: See p. 58.

DAY 5

9. International Bagels 40 MIN. INDIVIDUAL / PAIR

Materials: *craft dough or clay and encyclopedia*

You may want to have children ask classmates from different countries to tell them about foods in their culture. (Social Studies)

10. Food Safety 30 MIN. INDIVIDUAL / PAIR

Materials: *poster board, crayons, and markers*

Display posters around the classroom. (Health)

> ### Additional Activities
> • Anthology, pp. 178–179, Responding • TE p. R7, R9, R21, R29, R38, R40
> • Practice Book, p. 106, Grammar • Technology: See p. 58.

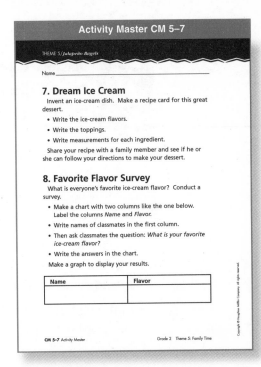

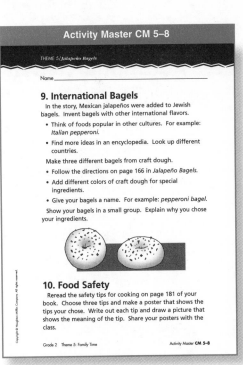

THEME 5/SELECTION 3: *Carousel*

Assignments for Independent Activities

Assign for On-Level Students

Masters: CM 5-9—CM 5-12

Teacher support: GO-1, GO-3, GO-8

Classroom materials: Construction paper, crayons, markers, scissors, drawing paper, globe, encyclopedia, poster board

Note: Many activities are appropriate for Extra Support students and English Language Learners.

Assign for Challenge Students

Masters: CH 5-5, CH 5-6

Teacher support: GO-1, GO-4

Classroom materials: See list of materials with each activity.

Note: Many activities are appropriate for advanced English Language Learners.

Check that students have read the selection or leveled reading specified for an activity.

- Anthology, pp. 184–221: *Carousel;* "Carousel Designed by Kids"

- Phonics Library: *Aunt Lizzy Finds Her Cake; My Brother*

- Theme Paperbacks: *Swim, Dad!* (On My Way Practice Reader); *Tonight is Carnival* (On Level); *Grandaddy and Janetta* (Challenge)

Provide copies of activity masters, graphic organizer masters, and challenge masters, as needed.

Additional Activities and Program Resources

Additional independent activities for this selection:

- Practice Book, pp. 109, 110, 114, 118, 119, 120, 122, 123, 124, 237

- Teacher's Resources Blackline Masters, Theme 5 Reading Cards 10, 11, 12

- TE pp. R11, R13, R23, R31, R39, R41

- TE Challenge pp. 214, 221, 221H, R11, R13, R23, R31, R38, R39, R40

Other program resources:

- Suggested in activities for this selection: Houghton Mifflin Social Studies Bookshelf: *It Takes a Village; Dear Annie*

- Students' self-selected independent reading materials

- Students' journals or other independent writing materials

Get Set to Read *Carousel*

Education Place: www.eduplace.com for more activities related to *Carousel*

Accelerated Reader®, *Carousel*

Audiotape, *Carousel*

Extra Support lessons for *Carousel*

English language development lessons for *Carousel*

DAY 1

Preteach Phonics: Sound of *y* at the End of Longer Words

Preteach Phonics: The Prefix *un-*

Preview *Aunt Lizzy Finds Her Cake*

- ES Handbook pp. 172–173 and masters PMES 5-5, TMES 5-5

Preteach Chores

Preteach Teacher Read Aloud *Great-Aunt Martha*

Preteach Structural Analysis: The Prefix *un-*

- ELL Handbook pp. 176–177 and master ELL 5-7

DAY 2

Preteach Comprehension: Making Judgments

Preview Selection, Segment 1

- ES Handbook pp. 174–175 and masters PMES 5-6, TMES 5-6

Preteach Moods

Preteach Get Set to Read; Anthology Selection

Reteach High-Frequency Words: *aunt*

- ELL Handbook pp. 178–179

DAY 3

Reteach High-Frequency Words

Reteach Grammar: Verbs That Tell About the Past

Preview Selection, Segment 2

- ES Handbook pp. 176–177

Preteach Zoo Animals

Reteach Phonics Review: The *-le* Ending in Two-Syllable Words

Reteach High-Frequency Words: *million, pair*

- ELL Handbook pp. 180–181

DAY 4

Reteach Phonics: Sound of *y* at the End of Longer Words

Reteach Phonics: The Prefix *un-*

Preview *My Brother*

- ES Handbook pp. 178–179

Preteach Repairs

Reteach Selection Summary and Review

Reteach Vocabulary: Homophones

- ELL Handbook pp. 182–183 and master ELL 5-8

DAY 5

Reteach Comprehension: Making Judgments

Revisit Selection, *Aunt Lizzy Finds Her Cake*, and *My Brother*

- ES Handbook pp. 180–181

Reteach Clothes and Shoes

Reteach Grammar: Verbs That Tell About the Past

Reteach Writing: Combining Sentences

- ELL Handbook pp. 184–185

DAY 1

1. *Aunt Lizzie Finds Her Cake* (Phonics Library)
40 MIN. INDIVIDUAL / PAIR

Materials: *construction paper, crayons, markers, and scissors*

Be sure that children understand that the first three clues should lead to the other clues and only the final clue should lead to the cake.

2. Fun Fair! 30 MIN. INDIVIDUAL / PAIR
Materials: *Graphic Organizer Master 1*
Explain that fairs and amusement parks have common features, but fairs are community-based and more family-oriented. Have children give examples of events in their community. (Social Studies)

Additional Activities

• Audio Tape, *Carousel*
• Practice Book, pp. 109, 110, Phonics
• Practice Book, p. 237, Spelling
• Technology: See p. 62.

DAY 2

3. Your Favorite Gift 30 MIN. INDIVIDUAL / PAIR
Materials: *drawing paper, crayons, and markers*

Display children's drawings on a classroom bulletin board.

4. Spelling Game 30 MIN. PAIR
Extend this activity by having children make cards for other spelling words.

Additional Activities

• Practice Book, p. 114, Comprehension
• Practice Book, p. 118, Spelling
• Practice Book, p. 122, Grammar
• Technology: See p. 62.

DAY 3

5. Thank You! 30 MIN. INDIVIDUAL
Ask volunteers to share their thank-you notes with the class.

6. You're Invited! <u>30 MIN.</u>   INDIVIDUAL

Materials: construction paper, markers and crayons

If necessary, review how to write dates and times. (Social Studies)

Additional Activities
- Practice Book, p. 119, Spelling
- Technology: See p. 62.

DAY 4

7. Carousel Critter   <u>30 MIN.</u>   INDIVIDUAL

Materials: construction paper, drawing paper, scissors, crayons, and markers

Take a class vote on the top three critters to be added to a carousel.

8. Alex's Carousel   <u>30 MIN.</u>   INDIVIDUAL

You may want to show Transparency 5-29 to children as an example of an information paragraph. (Social Studies)

Additional Activities
- Practice Book, p. 120, Spelling
- Practice Book, p. 123, Grammar
- Technology: See p. 62.

DAY 5

9. Wild Safari   <u>40 MIN.</u>   INDIVIDUAL / PAIR

Materials: globe, encyclopedia, poster board, markers and crayons

Hang children's posters around the classroom. (Science)

English Language Learners Have children work in pairs or in a small group.

10. Change It! Game   <u>20 MIN.</u>   PAIR / SMALL GROUP

If necessary, review rules for past and present verb tenses. Give several examples.

English Language Learners Pair up children with fluent English speakers.

Additional Activities
- Anthology, pp. 216–217, Responding
- Practice Book, p. 124, Grammar
- TE p. R11, R13, R23, R31, R39, R41
- Technology: See p. 62.

Activity Master CM 5–11

THEME 5/*Carousel*

Name _____

6. You're Invited!
Make an invitation to a party with a fair theme.
- Fold a sheet of construction paper in half to make a card.
- Draw a picture on the cover. Show one of the fun games or rides at the party.
Write details about the party inside the invitation. Include the following:
- the reason for the party, such as a birthday or summer vacation
- the date and time of the party
- the location
Pass your invitation around for classmates to read. Describe what special attractions and games will be at the party.

7. Carousel Critter
What animal would you like to see on a carousel? Design a new carousel critter. Use your imagination. Draw a picture of your new carousel critter. Write under the picture why you chose that critter and why you think it would be a good addition to a carousel. Share your drawing and ideas with the class.

CM 5–11 Activity Master   Grade 2   Theme 5: Family Time

Activity Master CM 5–12

THEME 5/*Carousel*

Name _____

8. Alex's Carousel
Write an information paragraph about Alex's carousel.
- Begin with a topic sentence that tells what the paragraph is about. Indent the first word.
- Then write four sentences about the topic.
- Look at a picture of Alex's carousel to remember details.
Read your paragraph to a classmate.

9. Wild Safari
Imagine that a carousel company wants you to go on an African safari. Your job is to observe animals that would be good for their new African carousel. Look for animals only found in Africa. Use an encyclopedia to help you. Make a poster of three animals that you are recommending. Draw each animal. Write two sentences about why you chose that animal. Share your poster with the class.

10. Change It! Game
Play Change It! with a classmate.
- Player 1 says an animal sentence using a past-tense verb. For example: *The tiger jumped.*
- Player 2 changes the sentence to include a present-tense verb. For example: *The tiger jumps.*
- Play until each of you has made ten sentences.

Grade 2   Theme 5: Family Time   Activity Master **CM 5–12**

THEME 5/SELECTION 4: *Thunder Cake*

Assignments for Independent Activities

Assign for On-Level Students

Masters: CM 5-13—CM 5-16

Teacher support: GO-1, GO-3, GO-8

Classroom materials: See also materials with each activity.

Note: Many activities are appropriate for Extra Support students and English Language Learners.

Check that students have read the selection or leveled reading specified for an activity.

- Anthology, pp. 224–261: *Thunder Cake;* "Sun and Ice"
- Phonics Library: *Eight Daughters!; The Family Garden*

Assign for Challenge Students

Masters: CH 5-7, CH 5-8

Teacher support: GO-1, GO-4

Classroom materials: Chart paper, calendar, encyclopedia and/or geography book, markers and crayons, drawing paper

Note: Many activities are appropriate for advanced English Language Learners.

- Theme Paperbacks: *Swim, Dad!* (On My Way Practice Reader); *Tonight is Carnival* (On Level); *Grandaddy and Janetta* (Challenge)

Provide copies of activity masters, graphic organizer masters, and challenge masters, as needed.

Additional Activities and Program Resources

Additional independent activities for this selection:

- Practice Book, pp. 127, 132, 136, 137, 138, 140, 141, 142, 238
- Teacher's Resources Blackline Masters, Theme 5 Reading Cards 14, 15, 16
- TE pp. R15, R17, R25, R33, R39, R41
- TE Challenge pp. 236, 249, 254, 261, 261H, 263, R15, R17, R25, R33, R39

Other program resources:

- Suggested in activities for this selection: Houghton Mifflin Social Studies Bookshelf: *It Takes a Village; Dear Annie*
- Students' self-selected independent reading materials
- Students' journals or other independent writing materials

 **Technology**

Get Set to Read *Thunder Cake*

Education Place: www.eduplace.com for more activities related to *Thunder Cake*

Accelerated Reader®, *Thunder Cake*

Audiotape, *Thunder Cake*

Extra Support lessons for *Thunder Cake*

English language development lessons for *Thunder Cake*

DAY 1

Preteach Structural Analysis: Base Words and *-ed, -ing* Endings
Preteach Phonics: Silent Consonants *gh, k* in *kn,* and *b* in *mb*
Preview *Eight Daughters*
  • ES Handbook pp. 182–183 and masters PMES 5–7, TMES 5–7

Preteach Special Occasions
Preteach Teacher Read Aloud *Sophie's Special Sponge Cake*
Preteach Phonics: Silent Consonants *gh, kn, b*
  • ELL Handbook pp. 186–187 and master ELL 5–10

DAY 2

Preteach Comprehension: Sequence of Events
Preview Selection, Segment 1
  • ES Handbook pp. 184–185 and masters PMES 5–8, TMES 5–8

Preteach Storms
Preteach Get Set to Read; Anthology Selection
Reteach High-Frequency Words: *air, child*
  • ELL Handbook pp. 188–189

DAY 3

Reteach High-Frequency Words
Reteach Grammar: Verbs *is/are, was/were*
Preview Selection, Segment 2
  • ES Handbook pp. 186–187

Preteach Places on a Farm
Reteach Phonics Review: Sound of *y* at the End of Longer Words
Reteach High-Frequency Words: *heavy, hour*
  • ELL Handbook pp. 190–191

DAY 4

Reteach Phonics: Base Words and Endings *-ed, -ing*
Reteach Phonics: Silent Consonants *gh, kn,* and *b* in *mb*
Preview *The Family Garden*
  • ES Handbook pp. 188–189

Preteach Time
Reteach Selection Summary and Review
Reteach Vocabulary/Dictionary: Finding Words with Endings
  • ELL Handbook pp. 192–193 and master ELL 5–11

DAY 5

Reteach Comprehension: Sequence of Events
Revisit Selection, *Eight Daughters,* and *The Family Garden*
  • ES Handbook pp. 190–191

Reteach Numerals and Number
Reteach Grammar: The Verbs *is/are, was/were*
Reteach Writing: Capitalization and Punctuation with Quotation Marks
  • ELL Handbook pp. 194–195

Activity Master CM 5–13

THEME 5/*Thunder Cake*

Name _____

1. The Cook's Helper
In *Sophie's Special Cake*, Sophie bakes a cake with help from her Nanny. Do you like to cook? Do you help in the kitchen at home?

• Write one thing you like to do in the kitchen.
• Write the steps for this activity.
• Use sequence words: *first, next, then, finally.*

Tell a classmate what you like to do in the kitchen. Explain your steps in the correct sequence.

2. Family Quilt
Look at the picture on page 229 in *Thunder Cake*. There's a colorful quilt. A *quilt* is a blanket made from squares with different designs. Make a family quilt from paper.

• Cut a sheet of construction paper into as many squares as you have family members. Include extended family and pets if you wish.
• Think of a design for each member of your family. You can use letters, names, numbers, shapes, or patterns.
• Draw one design on each square.
• Arrange the squares on another sheet of construction paper. When you decide on the arrangement or pattern you want, glue on the squares to make a "quilt."

Show your quilt to a classmate. Explain the meaning of each square.

CM 5–13 Activity Master   Grade 2 · Theme 5: Family Time

Activity Master CM 5–14

THEME 5/*Thunder Cake*

Name _____

3. Poem to a Storm
Storms can be very noisy. Write a poem about a noisy storm.

• Use words that sound like noises. For example: *rumble.*
• Write at least four phrases or sentences.
• Use exclamation marks for some noisy words.
• Write *very* noisy words in capital letters.

Read your poem to a classmate.

4. Storm Encounters
Have you ever experienced a storm? Write a personal narrative about what the storm was like and how you felt during it. Be sure to

• use personal pronouns like *I, we,* and *they*
• write about events in the order they happened

5. Rainy Day Fun
In *Thunder Cake*, the characters make a cake to entertain themselves during a storm. Imagine that your family is bored because it's raining. Think of ways to entertain them!

• Think of an activity your family can do indoors.
• Think of what your whole family likes to do.
• Then write how each family member can participate.

Share your ideas with your family.

Grade 2 · Theme 5: Family Time   Activity Master **CM 5–14**

DAY 1

1. The Cook's Helper <u>30 MIN.</u> INDIVIDUAL
Tell children that the activity can be very simple, such as putting away dishes. Explain that it can also be an occasional activity, such as watering the plants. (Social Studies)

English Language Learners Before writing, ask children to share ideas about things they like to do around the house

2. Family Quilt <u>30 MIN.</u> INDIVIDUAL / PAIR
Materials: construction paper, scissors, markers, crayons, and glue

Tell children they can draw objects that have special meaning to family members. (Social Studies) (Math)

> ### Additional Activities
> • Audio Tape, *Thunder Cake*
> • Practice Book, p. 127, Phonics
> • Practice Book, p. 238, Spelling
> • Technology: See p. 66.

DAY 2

3. Poem to a Storm <u>20 MIN.</u> INDIVIDUAL / PAIR
Tell students to use words that are less "noisy," such as those describing soft rain (*pitter patter*) or the wind (*whoosh*). (Science)

English Language Learners Have children work in pairs to brainstorm "noise" words.

4. Storm Encounters <u>30 MIN.</u> INDIVIDUAL
If children haven't been in a storm, tell them to use their imagination.

> ### Additional Activities
> • Practice Book, p. 132, Comprehension
> • Practice Book, p. 136, Spelling
> • Practice Book, p. 140, Grammar
> • Technology: See p. 66.

DAY 3

5. Rainy Day Fun <u>30 MIN.</u> INDIVIDUAL / PAIR
Tell children to think not only of games, but also household chores such as baking cookies or making crafts. (Social Studies)

6. Me and Babushka <u>40 MIN.</u> PAIR

Tell children to say their lines loudly and slowly. (Social Studies)

English Language Learners Tell children they can use phrases or sentences from the story if they wish.

> ### Additional Activities
> - Practice Book, p. 137, Spelling
> - Technology: See p. 66.

DAY 4

7. Sun and Ice <u>30 MIN.</u> INDIVIDUAL / PAIR

Materials: encyclopedia and/or geography book, chart paper, markers and crayons

Ask volunteers to share their charts with the class. (Science)

8. *The Family Garden* (Phonics Library) <u>30 MIN.</u> INDIVIDUAL

Materials: Graphic Organizer Master 3

If necessary, review story maps with children.

> ### Additional Activities
> - Practice Book, p. 138, Spelling
> - Practice Book, p. 141, Grammar
> - Technology: See p. 66.

DAY 5

9. My Favorite Season <u>30 MIN.</u> INDIVIDUAL

Materials: poster paper, markers and crayons

Tell children to think of the family activity before they draw. (Social Studies) (Science)

English Language Learners Encourage children from different countries to include plants and animals that might be native to their places of birth.

10. Acrostic Game <u>30 MIN.</u> PAIR

Illustrate how to structure an acrostic poem on the board.

> ### Additional Activities
> - Anthology, pp. 256–257, Responding
> - Practice Book, p. 142, Grammar
> - TE p. R15, R17, R25, R33, R39, R41
> - Technology: See p. 66.

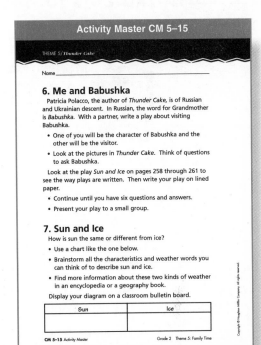

Activity Master CM 5–15

THEME 5/*Thunder Cake*

Name _____

6. Me and Babushka
Patricia Polacco, the author of *Thunder Cake*, is of Russian and Ukrainian descent. In Russian, the word for Grandmother is *Babushka*. With a partner, write a play about visiting Babushka.
- One of you will be the character of Babushka and the other will be the visitor.
- Look at the pictures in *Thunder Cake*. Think of questions to ask Babushka.

Look at the play *Sun and Ice* on pages 258 through 261 to see the way plays are written. Then write your play on lined paper.
- Continue until you have six questions and answers.
- Present your play to a small group.

7. Sun and Ice
How is sun the same or different from ice?
- Use a chart like the one below.
- Brainstorm all the characteristics and weather words you can think of to describe sun and ice.
- Find more information about these two kinds of weather in an encyclopedia or a geography book.

Display your diagram on a classroom bulletin board.

Sun	Ice

CM 5–15 Activity Master   Grade 2   Theme 5: Family Time

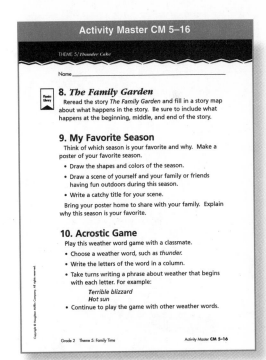

Activity Master CM 5–16

THEME 5/*Thunder Cake*

Name _____

8. *The Family Garden*
Reread the story *The Family Garden* and fill in a story map about what happens in the story. Be sure to include what happens at the beginning, middle, and end of the story.

9. My Favorite Season
Think of which season is your favorite and why. Make a poster of your favorite season.
- Draw the shapes and colors of the season.
- Draw a scene of yourself and your family or friends having fun outdoors during this season.
- Write a catchy title for your scene.

Bring your poster home to share with your family. Explain why this season is your favorite.

10. Acrostic Game
Play this weather word game with a classmate.
- Choose a weather word, such as *thunder*.
- Write the letters of the word in a column.
- Take turns writing a phrase about weather that begins with each letter. For example:
  > *Terrible blizzard*
  > *Hot sun*
- Continue to play the game with other weather words.

Grade 2   Theme 5: Family Time   Activity Master CM 5–16

THEME 6/SELECTION 1: *The Art Lesson*

Assignments for Independent Activities

Assign for On-Level Students

Classroom Management Handbook

Masters: CM 6–1—CM 6–4

Teacher support: GO–1, GO–6

Classroom materials: See list of materials with each activity.

Note: Many activities are appropriate for Extra Support students and English Language Learners.

Assign for Challenge Students

Challenge Handbook

Masters: CH 6–1, CH 6–2

Teacher support: GO–6

Classroom materials: Glue, poster board, encyclopedia, Internet access, construction paper, crayons, markers

Note: Many activities are appropriate for advanced English Language Learners.

Check that students have read the selection or leveled reading specified for an activity.

- Anthology, pp. 292–325: *The Art Lesson;* "Carmen Lomas Garza"
- Phonics Library: *Our Classroom Zoo Book; Jade's Drumming*

• Theme Paperbacks: *The Garden County Fair* (On My Way Practice Reader); *Annie's Gifts* (On Level); *Spotlight on Cody* (Challenge)

Provide copies of activity masters, graphic organizer masters, and challenge masters, as needed.

Additional Activities and Program Resources

Additional independent activities for this selection:

- Practice Book, pp. 155, 159, 163, 164, 165, 167, 168, 169, 239
- Teacher's Resources Blackline Masters, Theme 6 Reading Cards 2, 3, 4
- TE pp. R5, R11, R17, R25, R28
- TE Challenge pp. 285, 318, 325, 325H, R5, R11, R17, R25

Other program resources:

- Students' self-selected independent reading materials
- Students' journals or other independent writing materials

Technology

Get Set to Read *The Art Lesson*

Education Place: www.eduplace.com for more activities related to *The Art Lesson*

Accelerated Reader®, *The Art Lesson*

Audiotape, *The Art Lesson*

Extra Support lessons for *The Art Lesson*

English language development lessons for *The Art Lesson*

DAY 1

Preteach Phonics: Vowel pairs *oo, ew*
Preview *Our Classroom Zoo Book*
- ES Handbook pp. 194–195 and masters PMES 6-1, TMES 6-1

Preteach Winter Sports
Preteach Teacher Read Aloud *Omar on Ice*
Preteach Phonics: Vowel Pairs *oo, ew, ue, ou*
- ELL Handbook pp. 198–199 and master ELL 6-1

DAY 2

Preteach Author's Viewpoint
Preview Selection, Segment 1
- ES Handbook pp. 196–197 and masters PMES 6-2, TMES 6-2

Preteach People and Places in a School
Preteach Get Set to Read; Anthology Selection
Reteach High-Frequency Words: *fair*
- ELL Handbook pp. 200–201

DAY 3

Reteach High-Frequency Words
Reteach Irregular Forms of Verbs
Preview Selection, Segment 2
- ES Handbook pp. 198–199

Preteach School Subjects
Reteach Structural Analysis: Base Words and *-ed, -ing* Endings
Reteach High-Frequency Words: *gold, woman*
- ELL Handbook pp. 202–203

DAY 4

Reteach Phonics: Vowel Pairs *oo, ew, ue, ou*
Preview *Jade's Drumming*
- ES Handbook pp. 200–201

Preteach Grade Levels in School
Reteach Selection Summary and Review
Reteach Vocabulary: Word Families
- ELL Handbook pp. 204–205 and master ELL 6-2

DAY 5

Reteach Author's Viewpoint
Revisit Selection, *Jade's Drumming*, and *Our Classroom Zoo Book*
- ES Handbook pp. 202–203

Reteach Art Words
Reteach Grammar: Other Irregular Verbs
Reteach Writing: Is It a Sentence?
- ELL Handbook pp. 206–207

SELECTION 1:
The Art Lesson

Activities

DAY 1

1. Still Life 30 MIN. INDIVIDUAL / PAIR
Materials: drawing paper, crayons, and markers

Show examples of still life art by famous painters. Tell children that some views of their still life may not be suitable to draw because objects may be blocked.

English Language Learners Have children work in a small group.

2. -ING Words 30 MIN. PAIR / SMALL GROUP
Tell children if they are not sure about the action in a picture, they can describe the character's thoughts with action words.

> **Additional Activities**
> - Audio Tape, *The Art Lesson*
> - Practice Book, p. 155, Phonics
> - Practice Book, p. 239, Spelling
> - Technology: See p. 70.

DAY 2

3. *The Garden County Fair*
(On My Way Practice Reader) 40 MIN. INDIVIDUAL / PAIR
Materials poster paper, crayons, and markers

Explain the purpose of a time line. Review with children the concept of sequence.

4. Connect-a-Dot 20 MIN. PAIR
Materials: white tissue paper or tracing paper

Tell children to wait for instructions before they connect one dot to another. They must follow the numbers.

> **Additional Activities**
> - Practice Book, p. 159, Comprehension
> - Practice Book, p. 163, Spelling
> - Practice Book, p. 167, Grammar
> - Technology: See p. 70.

DAY 3

5. Try This 30 MIN. INDIVIDUAL / PAIR
Materials: Graphic Organizer Master 6

Explain to children that there are many possible solutions. Have children discuss the events in each picture.

Activity Master CM 6–1

THEME 6/*The Art Lesson*

Name_____

1. Still Life
Look at the picture on page 295 of *The Art Lesson*. The children are painting a still life. A *still life* is a painting of objects. Make some still life groupings. Collect at least six objects. Group the objects on a table in an interesting way. Ask a classmate to join you to talk about your still life.
- Walk around the table and stop four times. Talk about how the still life looks each time.
- Give your opinion of which view is best for a painting.
Now each of you should draw the still life from your favorite view.

2. -ING Words
Play this word game with a classmate.
- One player points to a person in a picture in *The Art Lesson*.
- The other player tells what the person is doing. The player must say only one word and it must end in -*ing*.
- Take turns finding pictures and saying -*ing* words.

CM 6–1 Activity Master Grade 2 Theme 6: Talent Show

Activity Master CM 6–2

THEME 6/*The Art Lesson*

Name_____

3. *The Garden County Fair*
Create a time line of events in *The Garden County Fair*.
- Look at the pictures in the story.
- List the events of the fair in order.
- Make a time line of the events for the day on a poster.
You can add pictures to your time line if you wish.

4. Connect-a-Dot
Prepare an art game to play with a classmate.
- Draw an object on a sheet of paper.
- Place white tissue paper over the drawing.
- Use a marker to make a connect-a-dot picture. Dab dots along the lines of the drawing underneath.
- Number the dots, starting with the number 1.
Give your dot picture to a classmate. Tell your classmate to connect the dots by following the numbers.

5. Try This
Find solutions to the problems in *The Art Lesson*.
- Use a Problem/Solution chart.
- Look at the pictures on pages 302 and 303.
- On your chart, write the problem you see in each picture.
- Write your own solution.
Talk about the events in each picture with a classmate.

Grade 2 Theme 6: Talent Show Activity Master CM 6–2

72 THEME 6: **Talent Show**

English Language Learners Have them work in pairs. Tell them they can use phrases or sentences from the story, if they wish.

6. Word Search   30 MIN.   INDIVIDUAL / PAIR

Materials: graph paper

Review how to construct a word search game. Ask children to make a list of art words before they create the game.

Additional Activities
- Practice Book, p. 164, Spelling
- Technology: See p. 70.

DAY 4

7. Artist   30 MIN.   INDIVIDUAL / PAIR

Ask volunteers to share their paragraphs with the class.

English Language Learners Have them work in pairs.

8. Dear Miss Landers   30 MIN.   PAIR / SMALL GROUP

Display letters on a classroom bulletin board.

Additional Activities
- Practice Book, p. 165, Spelling
- Practice Book, p. 168, Grammar
- Technology: See p. 70.

DAY 5

9. My Portrait   30 MIN.   INDIVIDUAL

Materials: small mirror (optional)

Instruct children to draw a portrait that expresses action or feelings.

English Language Learners: Have children share portraits with each other.

10. Carmen Lomas Garza   30 MIN.   INDIVIDUAL

Materials: encyclopedia and art books

Ask volunteers to share their paragraphs with the class.

Additional Activities
- Anthology, pp. 320–321, Responding
- Practice Book, p. 169, Grammar
- TE p. R5, R11, R17, R25, R28
- Technology: See p. 70.

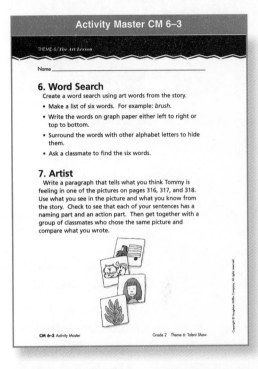

Activity Master CM 6–3

THEME 6/ *The Art Lesson*

Name_____

6. Word Search
Create a word search using art words from the story.
- Make a list of six words. For example: *brush.*
- Write the words on graph paper either left to right or top to bottom.
- Surround the words with other alphabet letters to hide them.
- Ask a classmate to find the six words.

7. Artist
Write a paragraph that tells what you think Tommy is feeling in one of the pictures on pages 316, 317, and 318. Use what you see in the picture and what you know from the story. Check to see that each of your sentences has a naming part and an action part. Then get together with a group of classmates who chose the same picture and compare what you wrote.

CM 6–3 Activity Master   Grade 2   Theme 6: Talent Show

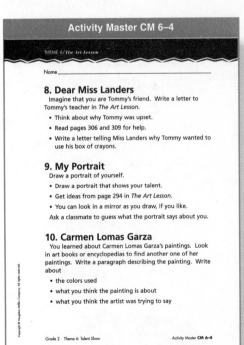

Activity Master CM 6–4

THEME 6/ *The Art Lesson*

Name_____

8. Dear Miss Landers
Imagine that you are Tommy's friend. Write a letter to Tommy's teacher in *The Art Lesson.*
- Think about why Tommy was upset.
- Read pages 306 and 309 for help.
- Write a letter telling Miss Landers why Tommy wanted to use his box of crayons.

9. My Portrait
Draw a portrait of yourself.
- Draw a portrait that shows your talent.
- Get ideas from page 294 in *The Art Lesson.*
- You can look in a mirror as you draw, if you like.
Ask a classmate to guess what the portrait says about you.

10. Carmen Lomas Garza
You learned about Carmen Lomas Garza's paintings. Look in art books or encyclopedias to find another one of her paintings. Write a paragraph describing the painting. Write about
- the colors used
- what you think the painting is about
- what you think the artist was trying to say

Grade 2   Theme 6: Talent Show   Activity Master CM 6–4

THEME 6/SELECTION 2: *Moses Goes to a Concert*

Assignments for Independent Activities

Assign for On-Level Students

Masters: CM 6-5—CM 6-8

Teacher support: GO-6, GO-10

Classroom materials: See list of materials with each activity.

Note: Many activities are appropriate for Extra Support students and English Language Learners.

Assign for Challenge Students

Masters: CH 6-3, CH 6-4

Teacher support: GO-6

Classroom materials: Encyclopedia, poster board, crayons, markers, index cards, a copy of the alphabet in sign language

Note: Many activities are appropriate for advanced English Language Learners.

Check that students have read the selection or leveled reading specified for an activity.

- Anthology, pp. 330–369: *Moses Goes to a Concert;* "Go to a Concert"
- Phonics Library: *Dwight the Knight; Who Drew the Cartoon?*

- Theme Paperbacks: *The Garden County Fair* (On My Way Practice Reader); *Annie's Gifts* (On Level); *Spotlight on Cody* (Challenge)

Provide copies of activity masters, graphic organizer masters, and challenge masters, as needed.

Additional Activities and Program Resources

Additional independent activities for this selection:

- Practice Book, pp. 177, 181, 184, 185, 186, 187, 189, 190, 191, 241
- Teacher's Resources Blackline Masters, Theme 6 Reading Cards 6, 7, 8
- TE pp. R7, R13, R19, R26, R28
- TE Challenge pp. 362, 369, 369H, R7, R13, R19, R26

Other program resources:

- Students' self-selected independent reading materials
- Students' journals or other independent writing materials

Technology

Get Set to Read *Moses Goes to a Concert*

Education Place: www.eduplace.com for more activities related to *Moses Goes to a Concert*

Accelerated Reader®, *Moses Goes to a Concert*

Audiotape, *Moses Goes to a Concert*

Extra Support lessons
for *Moses Goes to a Concert*

English language development lessons
for *Moses Goes to a Concert*

DAY 1

Preteach Phonics: Long *i (igh)*
Preview *Dwight the Knight*
- ES Handbook pp. 204–205 and masters PMES 6-3, TMES 6-3

Preteach Music Words
Preteach Teacher Read Aloud *Sam Sings*
Preteach Phonics: Long *i (igh, ie)*
- ELL Handbook pp. 208–209 and master ELL 6-4

DAY 2

Preteach Noting Details
Preview Selection, Segment 1
- ES Handbook pp. 206–207 and masters PMES 6-4, TMES 6-4

Preteach Audience Behavior
Preteach Get Set to Read; Anthology Selection
Reteach High-Frequency Words: *alphabet*
- ELL Handbook pp. 210–211

DAY 3

Reteach High-Frequency Words
Reteach Adjectives, including *a, an,* and *the*
Preview Selection, Segment 2
- ES Handbook pp. 208–209

Preteach Instrument Families
Reteach Phonics Review: Vowel Pairs *oo, ew, ue, ou*
Reteach High-Frequency Words: *heart, mind*
- ELL Handbook pp. 212–213

DAY 4

Reteach Phonics: Long *i (igh, ie)*
Preview *Who Drew the Cartoon?*
- ES Handbook pp. 210–211

Preteach Jobs and Careers
Reteach Selection Summary and Review
Reteach Vocabulary: Multiple-Meaning Words
- ELL Handbook pp. 214–215 and master ELL 6-5

DAY 5

Reteach Noting Details
Revisit Selection, *Moses Goes to a Concert, Dwight the Knight,* and *Who Drew the Cartoon?*
- ES Handbook pp. 212–213

Reteach Performances
Reteach Grammar: Adjectives, including *a, an,* and *the*
Reteach Writing: Paraphrasing
- ELL Handbook pp. 216–217

Activities

Activity Master CM 6–5

THEME 6/*Moses Goes to a Concert*

Name _____

1. My Performance

In the story *Sam Sings*, Sam was afraid to sing by himself on stage, even though he sang all the time. Think about a time that you were asked to perform or do something in front of a large group. Were you afraid like Sam? What did you finally do? Write a journal entry about that experience.

 2. The Garden County Fair

Make a flyer to tell people about *The Garden County Fair*.

• There are many different things to do at a fair. Make a list of the different activities to include in your flyer.
• Draw pictures of the different events.
• Remember to tell when and where the fair is.
• You may also find more information in an encyclopedia.

Share your flyer with a classmate. Ask them what events they would like to go to at the fair.

**3. The Garden County Fair/
Annie's Gifts**

Read *The Garden County Fair* or *Annie's Gifts*. Write a short summary about the story:

• Tell about the characters and the setting.
• Describe the main story events.
• Write about the talent of the main character.

Retell the story in your own words to a classmate.

CM 6–5 Activity Master   Grade 2 Theme 6: Talent Show

Activity Master CM 6–6

THEME 6/*Moses Goes to a Concert*

Name _____

4. Sound Experiment

In *Moses Goes to a Concert*, you read about musical instruments. Conduct this sound experiment with a classmate.

• Find a book with a hard cover.
• Stretch a rubber band around the book, down the middle.
• Put two pencils under the band, one at each end.
• Pluck the band to make a sound.
• Try moving the pencils closer together. Does the sound change?
• Try plucking the band with a pick. Use a flat object. Does the sound change?

Now, write a paragraph telling what you learned about changes in sound.

5. Vowel Scene

• Draw a scene that contains four or five things with a long *i* sound, such as in *kite*.
• Next to each of those things write blanks for each letter in its name. For example, you would write _ _ _ _ by the picture of the kite. Write the words on the back of your paper.
• Trade scenes with a classmate. Each of you should try to fill in each other's picture. If you cannot tell what the picture is, ask your classmates for a clue.

Grade 2 Theme 6: Talent Show   Activity Master **CM 6–6**

DAY 1

1. My Performance 30 MIN. INDIVIDUAL

Ask volunteers to share their journal entries with the class.

2. *The Garden County Fair*
(On My Way Practice Reader) 30 MIN. PAIR / SMALL GROUP

Materials: construction paper and encyclopedia (optional)

Bring in an example of a flyer. Remind children to note details in the story to help them make their flyers.

> ### Additional Activities
>
> • Audio Tape, *Moses Goes to a Concert*
> • Practice Book, p. 177, Phonics
> • Practice Book, p. 241, Spelling
> • Technology: See p. 74.

DAY 2

3. *The Garden County Fair* (On My Way Practice Reader)/*Annie's Gifts* (On-Level Theme Paperback)

40 MIN. INDIVIDUAL/ PAIR

If necessary, show Transparency 6-19 to point out the features of a summary.

4. Sound Experiment 30 MIN. INDIVIDUAL / PAIR

Materials: thick rubber bands, wooden pencils, and hard cover books

Tell children to make sure there is space between the rubber band and the book cover. (Science)

English Language Learners Demonstrate the term *pluck*. Explain that a guitarist uses a pick to pluck the strings.

> ### Additional Activities
>
> • Practice Book, p. 181, Comprehension
> • Practice Book, p. 185, Spelling
> • Practice Book, p. 189, Grammar
> • Technology: See p. 74.

DAY 3

5. Vowel Scene 30 MIN. INDIVIDUAL / PAIR

Materials: drawing paper, crayons, and markers

Tell children they can check if their words have a long or short *i* sound in their Phonics book or a dictionary.

6. My Trip to a Concert <u>30 MIN.</u> INDIVIDUAL

Ask volunteers to share their stories with the class.

Additional Activities

- Practice Book, p. 186, Spelling
- Technology: See p. 74.

DAY 4

7. Shake It! <u>30 MIN.</u> INDIVIDUAL / PAIR

Materials: plastic cups; large quantities of small, hard objects; and poster paper

Have children sing a song as they use their shakers.

8. Sign It <u>30 MIN.</u> PAIR / SMALL GROUP

Make sure children do not copy the signed sentences.

Additional Activities

- Practice Book, p. 184, Phonics
- Practice Book, p. 187, Spelling
- Practice Book, p. 190, Grammar
- Technology: See p. 74.

DAY 5

9. Concert Tips <u>20 MIN.</u> INDIVIDUAL / PAIR

Materials: poster board, crayons, and markers

Tell children to categorize the tips before writing them on their posters.

10. Music Survey <u>40 MIN.</u> INDIVIDUAL / PAIR

Tell children to ask classmates to spell their favorite performer's name.

Additional Activities

- Anthology, pp. 364–365, Responding
- Practice Book, p. 191, Grammar
- TE p. R7, R13, R19, R26, R28
- Technology: See p. 74.

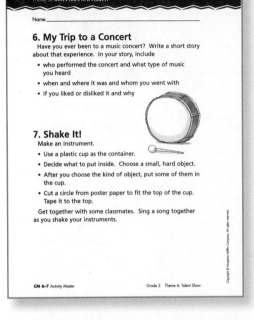

Activity Master CM 6–7

THEME 6/ *Moses Goes to a Concert*

Name _____

6. My Trip to a Concert
Have you ever been to a music concert? Write a short story about that experience. In your story, include
- who performed the concert and what type of music you heard
- when and where it was and whom you went with
- if you liked or disliked it and why

7. Shake It!
Make an instrument.
- Use a plastic cup as the container.
- Decide what to put inside. Choose a small, hard object.
- After you choose the kind of object, put some of them in the cup.
- Cut a circle from poster paper to fit the top of the cup. Tape it to the top.

Get together with some classmates. Sing a song together as you shake your instruments.

CM 6–7 Activity Master   Grade 2 Theme 6: Talent Show

Activity Master CM 6–8

THEME 6/ *Moses Goes to a Concert*

Name _____

8. Sign It
Look at the pictures of Moses and Ms. Elwyn using sign language in *Moses Goes to a Concert*. Create new sentences in sign language.
- First, write two sentences using words from the pictures.
- Then look for each word's sign. Practice signing the complete sentence.
- Sign the sentences for a classmate. Ask your classmate to guess the words as you sign.

9. Concert Tips
In the article "Go to a Concert," the author gives you tips on what to do at concerts. Make a poster that lists these tips. Draw pictures to go with the tips. Tell what kind of concert each tip is for. Share your poster with the class.

10. Music Survey
Who is everyone's favorite musical performer? Take a survey.
- Make a chart with three columns. Label the columns: *Student, Favorite Performer,* and *Details*.
- Ask classmates to name their favorite performer.
- Write the students' names in the first column.
- Write the performers' names in the second column.
- Write why they like the performer in the third column.
- Count the favorites and share the results.

Grade 2 Theme 6: Talent Show   Activity Master **CM 6–8**

THEME 6/SELECTION 3: *The School Mural*

Assignments for Independent Activities

Assign for On-Level Students

Classroom Management Handbook

Masters: CM 6-9—CM 6-12

Teacher support: GO-6, GO-10

Classroom materials: Drawing paper, crayons, markers

Note: Many activities are appropriate for Extra Support students and English Language Learners.

Check that students have read the selection or leveled reading specified for an activity.

- Anthology, pp. 372-397: *The School Mural*; "School Comics"
- Phonics Library: *Will Holly Sing?*; *Fright Night*

Assign for Challenge Students

Challenge Handbook

Masters: CH 6-5, CH 6-6

Teacher support: GO-6

Classroom materials: Drawing paper, crayons, markers

Note: Many activities are appropriate for advanced English Language Learners.

- Theme Paperbacks: *The Garden County Fair* (On My Way Practice Reader); *Annie's Gifts* (On Level); *Spotlight on Cody* (Challenge)

Provide copies of activity masters, graphic organizer masters, and challenge masters, as needed.

Additional Activities and Program Resources

Additional independent activities for this selection:

- Practice Book, pp. 194, 201, 202, 203, 204, 206, 207, 208, 241
- Teacher's Resources Blackline Masters, Theme 6 Reading Cards 10, 11, 12
- TE pp. R9, R15, R21, R27, R29
- TE Challenge pp. 392, 397, 397H, 399, R9, R15, R21, R25, R28, R29

Other program resources:

- Students' self-selected independent reading materials
- Students' journals or other independent writing materials

Get Set to Read *The School Mural*

Education Place: www.eduplace.com for more activities related to *The School Mural*

Accelerated Reader®, *The School Mural*

Audiotape, *The School Mural*

Extra Support lessons for *The School Mural*

 English language development lessons for *The School Mural*

DAY 1

Preteach More Words with *-ed* or *-ing*
Preview *Will Holly Sing?*
- ES Handbook pp. 214–215 and masters PMES 6-5, TMES 6-5

Preteach Working Together
Preteach Teacher Read Aloud *Mr. Mell Goes to Camp*
Preteach Phonics: More Words with *-ed* or *-ing*
- ELL Handbook pp. 218–219 and master ELL 6-7

DAY 2

Preteach Problem Solving
- ES Handbook pp. 216–217 and masters PMES 6-6, TMES 6-6

Preteach Numbers and Numerals from 50 to 100
Preteach Get Set to Read; Anthology Selection
Reteach High-Frequency Words: *below*
- ELL Handbook pp. 220–221

DAY 3

Reteach High-Frequency Words
Reteach Adjectives that Compare
Preview Selection, Segment 2
- ES Handbook pp. 218–219

Preteach Sections of the Newspaper
Reteach Phonics Review: Long *i (igh, ie)*
Reteach High-Frequency Words: *neighbor, should*
- ELL Handbook pp. 222–223

DAY 4

Reteach Phonics: Base Words and Endings *-ed, -ing*
- ES Handbook pp. 220–221

Preteach Symbols of School Pride
Reteach Selection Summary and Review
Reteach Vocabulary: Using Context
- ELL Handbook pp. 224–225 and master ELL 6-8

DAY 5

Reteach Problem Solving
Revisit *The School Mural, Fright Night,* and *Will Holly Sing?*
- ES Handbook pp. 222–223

Reteach Taking Turns
Reteach Grammar: Comparing with Adjectives
Reteach Writing: Giving Examples
- ELL Handbook pp. 226–227

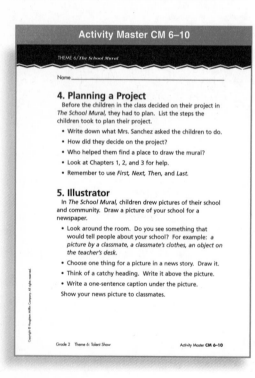

Activity Master CM 6–9

THEME 6/*The School Mural*

Name _____

1. What Happened?
Make a list of all the events that happened in the story *Mr. Mell Goes to Camp.* Then put the events in the order that they happened. Compare lists with a classmate.

2. *Will Holly Sing?*
At the end of the story *Will Holly Sing?*, Holly sings a song called "Good Friends" and dedicates it to Tom and Luke. Why does she do this? Write a short paragraph explaining Holly's choice.

3. Questions Game
Play this game with a classmate.
• Look through *The School Mural* to find illustrations.
• One player asks a question about the illustration.
• The other player answers the question.
Take turns asking questions. Check the answers by reading under each picture.

CM 6-9 Activity Master   Grade 2 Theme 6: Talent Show

Activity Master CM 6–10

THEME 6/*The School Mural*

Name _____

4. Planning a Project
Before the children in the class decided on their project in *The School Mural,* they had to plan. List the steps the children took to plan their project.
• Write down what Mrs. Sanchez asked the children to do.
• How did they decide on the project?
• Who helped them find a place to draw the mural?
• Look at Chapters 1, 2, and 3 for help.
• Remember to use *First, Next, Then,* and *Last.*

5. Illustrator
In *The School Mural,* children drew pictures of their school and community. Draw a picture of your school for a newspaper.
• Look around the room. Do you see something that would tell people about your school? For example: *a picture by a classmate, a classmate's clothes, an object on the teacher's desk.*
• Choose one thing for a picture in a news story. Draw it.
• Think of a catchy heading. Write it above the picture.
• Write a one-sentence caption under the picture.
Show your news picture to classmates.

Grade 2 Theme 6: Talent Show   Activity Master CM 6-10

DAY 1

1. What Happened? <u>30 MIN.</u> INDIVIDUAL/PAIR
Have children use their lists to retell the story.

2. *Will Holly Sing?* (Phonics Library) <u>30 MIN.</u> INDIVIDUAL
Ask volunteers to share their paragraphs with the class.

Additional Activities

• Audio Tape, *The School Mural*
• Practice Book, p. 194, Phonics
• Practice Book, p. 241 Spelling
• Technology: See p. 78.

DAY 2

3. Questions Game <u>30 MIN.</u> PAIR / SMALL GROUP
Instruct children to ask several questions about each illustration and to take turns asking and answering. The questions do not have to be related to the story events.

4. Planning a Project
You may wish to review the concept of *sequence.* Remind children how they have planned for projects in your own classroom.

English Language Learners Have them work in pairs. Tell them to use the author's sentences if they have difficulty.

Additional Activities

• Practice Book, p. 198, Comprehension
• Practice Book, p. 202, Spelling
• Practice Book, p. 206, Grammar
• Technology: See p. 78.

DAY 3

5. Illustrator <u>30 MIN.</u> INDIVIDUAL / PAIR
Show examples of photos and headings in a newspaper. Tell children to do a quick sketch as an idea for a photo.

English Language Learners Have children work in pairs.

6. Family Talent   30 MIN.   INDIVIDUAL

Materials: *Graphic Organizer Master 1*

Explain that talents can include something special about a person's character, such as telling jokes or being a good listener. (Social Studies)

Additional Activities
- Practice Book, p. 203, Spelling
- Technology: See p. 78.

DAY 4

7. It's Raining Inside!   30 MIN.   INDIVIDUAL

Tell children to think about as many solutions as possible. If there is additional time, have them draw their solution on paper.

8. Compare   30 MIN.   PAIR ICON / GROUP

Show Transparency 6-27 to review comparing with adjectives. Tell children comparing similar objects is only one kind of comparison. They can compare different objects by comparing features such as size, color, and shape.

Additional Activities
- Practice Book, p. 201, Phonics
- Practice Book, p. 204, Spelling
- Practice Book, p. 207, Grammar
- Technology: See p. 78.

DAY 5

9. School Murals   20 MIN.   INDIVIDUAL / PAIR

Materials: *Graphic Organizer Master 1*

Tell children to think of scenes for their murals that would brighten up or change the mood of a location. Children should also consider scenes that would illustrate something special about the school.

10. Hobbies   30 MIN.   INDIVIDUAL / PAIR

Materials: *drawing paper, crayons, and markers*

Display children's drawings around the classroom.

English Language Learners Explain the word *hobby* to children. Brainstorm a list of hobbies with them.

Additional Activities
- Anthology, pp. 394–395, Responding
- Practice Book, p. 208, Grammar
- TE p. R9, R15, R21, R27, R29
- Technology: See p. 78.

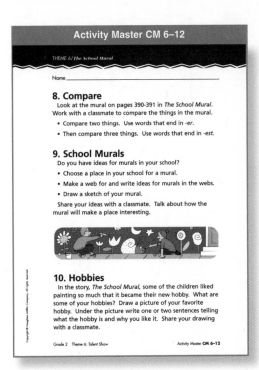

Activity Master CM 6–11

THEME 6/*The School Mural*

Name_____

6. Family Talent
What kind of talents does everyone have in your family?
- Make a web of your family and pets. In the center circle write *Family Talents*.
- Write one talent in the web for each family member. Include yourself.

Show the web to a classmate. Tell your classmate to ask questions about it.

7. It's Raining Inside!
Look at the *School Comics* on page 396. Can you help solve the problems? Make a *Solving Problems* chart like the one on page 197 in your Practice Book. Do these things for each problem:
- Write the problem in the first column.
- Think about as many ideas to solve the problem as you can. Write them down in the second column.
- Put the solution in the third column.

Share your solutions with a classmate. See if you have some of the same solutions.

CM 6–11 Activity Master   Grade 2   Theme 6: Talent Show

Activity Master CM 6–12

THEME 6/*The School Mural*

Name_____

8. Compare
Look at the mural on pages 390-391 in *The School Mural*. Work with a classmate to compare the things in the mural.
- Compare two things. Use words that end in *-er*.
- Then compare three things. Use words that end in *-est*.

9. School Murals
Do you have ideas for murals in your school?
- Choose a place in your school for a mural.
- Make a web for and write ideas for murals in the webs.
- Draw a sketch of your mural.

Share your ideas with a classmate. Talk about how the mural will make a place interesting.

10. Hobbies
In the story, *The School Mural*, some of the children liked painting so much that it became their new hobby. What are some of your hobbies? Draw a picture of your favorite hobby. Under the picture write one or two sentences telling what the hobby is and why you like it. Share your drawing with a classmate.

Grade 2   Theme 6: Talent Show   Activity Master **CM 6–12**

Blackline Masters for Grade 2

Activity Masters

Graphic Organizer Masters

Classroom Management Masters

Name_____

1. Imaginary Creatures

Compare and contrast Dragon with another imaginary creature that you have read about. Make two lists. Label the first list *Same,* the second *Different.* When writing words in your lists, think about

- how the creatures look and act
- where the creatures live
- what the creatures eat

Share your lists with the class.

2. Dragon's Lair

The dragon in *Dragon Gets By* lived in a house. But in most stories, dragons live in a cave called a *lair.* Make a list of animals. Then next to each animal write the name of the place where they live. If you need to, look up the animals' homes in an encyclopedia. When you finish your list, choose one animal and draw a picture of it living in its home. Under the picture, write a sentence that describes the animal and its home.

3. Silly Snack

Make up a recipe for a silly snack. Use your favorite foods as ingredients. For example: *peanut butter, apples,* and *raisins on a cracker.* Write your recipe on an index card. Show it to a classmate. Would he or she eat the snack? Why or why not?

4. Dragon Noises

Imagine the different sounds a dragon might make. Do its wings beat when it flies? Does it breathe fire? Working with a partner, create a list of six sound words that describe the sounds a dragon might make. Together, write sentences using the words in your list.

5. Make a Match!

Play this matching game with a classmate.

• Make a list of the vocabulary words and their meanings from *Dragon Gets By.* The words are on page 5 of the Practice Book. You will use this list as your answer key.

• Write each vocabulary word on an index card. Write each meaning on a different index card.

• Arrange the word cards face up on your desk. Place the meaning cards in a pile face down.

• Have a classmate choose a meaning card from the top of the pile and try to match it with a word. If the match is correct, he or she keeps the cards. If the match is incorrect, he or she places the meaning card on the bottom of the pile. Keep playing until all the meanings have been matched.

6. The Dragon's World

Imagine what life would be like if dragons were real and living near you, as in *Dragon Gets By.* Write a short story about meeting a dragon. Be sure to include

- a beginning, middle, and end to your story

- pictures for your story

7. Group Story

Create a group story about a dragon.

- One person in the group begins the story by saying a sentence.

- Each member of the group adds one sentence to the story, building on what has been said so far.

- The last sentence should be an ending to the story.

8. Food Phrases

Here's a game Dragon would love! It's all about food.

- Write ten food words on an index card.

- Exchange cards with a classmate.

- Make up a rhyme for each word on the card. Use a short phrase for each rhyme. For example, *dip the chip.* Write your rhyme on a separate sheet of paper.

- Share your rhymes with your classmate.

9. Grocery Riddles

Ask classmates to join you in this game. Think of a food you would find in a grocery store. Make up a riddle about the food. Your riddle should include clues about the food's

- size
- color
- texture
- taste

For example, *I am round and yummy. Sometimes I am green and sometimes I am red. I am crunchy and sweet.* (Answer: apple) See if your classmates can guess the name of the food. If no one guesses, add clues until someone gives the answer.

10. Follow That Dragon!

Create a chart showing the story structure of *Dragon Gets By.*

- Fold a piece of paper in half, and then in half again to create four boxes.

- In the first box, write a few sentences describing who is in the story and where the story takes place.

- In the second box, draw a picture of what happens at the beginning of the story. Write a sentence describing your picture.

- In the third box, draw and write about what happens at the middle of the story.

- In the fourth box, draw and write about what happens at the end of the story.

Share your chart with a classmate.

Name_____

1. Alaskan Animals

In the story *Julius*, Maya receives an Alaskan pig from her grandfather. What other kinds of animals live in Alaska?

- Look up Alaska in an encyclopedia or other reference source. Make a list of all the animals that live there. Note any important details you find about them.

- Choose one of those animals and draw a picture of it. Under your picture, write three or four sentences that talk about what Alaskan animal you chose and why.

Share your drawings with the class.

2. Pet Names

Julius is the name Maya gave her pet pig. What name would you give an unusual pet?

- Make a list of five unusual pets. For example: *elephant, monkey,* or *boa constrictor.*

- What if these animals were your pets? What names would you give them? Write your choices next to each animal. Choose your favorite unusual pet.

Write a letter to a friend telling him or her about your favorite new pet. In your letter, talk about

- where you keep it

- what you feed it

- what problems you have with it

- how you solve the problems

Name_____

3. Pig Riddles

Use the code to answer the following riddle:

A	B	C	D	E	F	G	H	I	J	K	L	M	N	O	P	Q	R	S	T	U	V	W	X	Y	Z
1	2	3	4	5	6	7	8	9	10	11	12	13	14	15	16	17	18	19	20	21	22	23	24	25	26

What kind of bath do pigs like?

8   15   7   23   1   19   8

___   ___   ___   ___   ___   ___   ___

Make a pig riddle of your own. Write the question on an index card. Draw a line for each letter of the answer. Write the code for the missing letters over the lines. Give your riddle to a classmate or family member to solve. If you need help, look up words in the dictionary that begin with *pig* or *hog.*

Theme Paperback

4. *Fluff and the Long Nap/The Adventures of Sugar and Junior*

Think about the main characters in either *Fluff and the Long Nap* or *The Adventures of Sugar and Junior.* What other adventures might they have? Write a new adventure for one of the stories. Before you write, first review the story and answer these questions:

- What will the setting be?

- What will happen in the new chapter? What is its plot?

- Will the new chapter be funny or serious? Will it include fantasy or realism?

Write your adventure. Trade stories with a classmate. Talk about what you liked about each other's work.

5. Fact or Fiction

Reread the story *Julius*. You know that most of what happens in this story is fantasy, or not real. But, there are some parts of the story that could happen. Working with a partner, fill-in a fantasy/realism chart for *Julius*. Then, rewrite the story so that all the parts listed in the fantasy column are real. Share your real stories with the class.

6. Silly Rhymes

Make a word web of words that rhyme with pig.

- Write *pig* in the center circle of the web. In all the other circles, write words that rhyme with *pig.*

- Once your web is done, choose a partner. Using both your webs, write two or three silly rhymes using the words.

7. Miss Manners

In the story *Julius,* Maya has to teach Julius some manners. What kinds of things does he need to learn?

- Reread the story *Julius.* Make a list of the manners you think Julius needs to learn.

- Create a chart by folding a sheet of paper in half lengthwise. On the left-hand side, write all the manners from your list.

- On the right-hand side, write how Julius could behave better.

8. Tricky Pictures

Choose one of your favorite silly stories from the classroom library—a story that made you laugh or smile. Look through the story and find your favorite picture. Write down all the details you can from that picture. Write five questions about what you see in that picture using those details. Trade your book and questions with a partner. See how many of the questions he or she can get right.

9. Fill It In!

Make a fill-in word game.

- Write your own sentence for each vocabulary word in *Julius.* The words are on page 27 of the Practice Book.

- Then on one side of an index card, copy the sentence leaving a blank where the vocabulary word goes.

- On the other side of the index card, write the vocabulary word that goes in the blank.

- Lay out your cards, sentence side up, on your desk. Ask a classmate to play the game by choosing the vocabulary word that best completes the sentence.

10. Postcard From Grandfather

In the story *Julius*, Maya's grandfather travels to Alaska every winter. Imagine that you are Maya's grandfather and you send her a postcard from Alaska. Find out about interesting places to visit in Alaska. Make a postcard of that place and write a short message on it that Maya's grandfather might have written to her.

Name _____

1. Silly Sentences

In *Mrs. Brown Goes to Town*, there are many animals that do silly things while she is away. Think about other animals that might live on her farm. Make a list of these animals. Write one silly sentences for each animal on your list. Write about what they might be doing while she is away. Share your sentences with a classmate.

2. Many Meanings

Some words look the same but have different meanings. The word *letter* is an example. *W* is a *letter* of the alphabet. A *letter* is also a written message you mail or send to someone, like what Mrs. Brown sent to her animals. How many words like letter can you find?

- With a partner, make a list of words that you think have two meanings. Use a dictionary to make sure that the words have two different meanings.

- Write two sentences for each word, one for each of its meaning. Share your sentences with the class.

3. Barnyard Poster

Think about all the different kinds of animals that live on a farm. Using pictures cut from old magazines, create a poster of barnyard animals. Put the animals where they might live on a farm and label them.

4. Caught in the Act!

Choose one of the pictures from *Mrs. Brown Went to Town* where the animals are doing something they should not be doing. Imagine that Mrs. Brown came home right at that moment. What would the animals do and say?

- Divide a piece of drawing paper in half.
- In one half, write what each of the animals are doing that they should not be doing.
- In the other half, write what you think the animal would say or do if Mrs. Brown came home and caught them.

5. Take a Vote

The animals in *Mrs. Brown Went to Town* took a vote. They voted to decide if they should live in the house. Take a vote in class.

- Make a chart with three columns. Label the first column *Action,* the second column *Yes,* and the third column *No.*
- Write an action in the *Action* column that you want the class to do. For example: *I want everyone to play baseball after school* or *Let's decorate the windows in the room.*
- Ask each student to vote on the action. They can say *yes* or *no* to your idea.
- Write the students' names in the correct column.
- Add up the votes in each column. How many yes votes are there? How many no votes?

6. Rhyming Circle

Did you notice the rhymes in *Mrs. Brown Went to Town?*
Sit in a circle and share a rhyme.

- The first person says a word. The person to his or her right says a word that rhymes with the first word. The next person says another word that rhymes.

- Continue until all players have said a rhyming word.

- Then the next person begins with a new word. Everyone takes turns saying rhyming words again.

- Continue the rhyming circle until all the members have introduced a new word.

7. Word Jumble

Follow these directions to play a jumble word game.

- Make a numbered list of all the vocabulary words on page 44 of the Practice Book.

- On the 2-inch squares of paper, write each letter from the first word on your list.

- On the backs of each of the letters of the word, write the number of the word. This is in case you forget which letters go with which words.

- Continue steps two and three until you have made letter squares for all the words.

- Mix up each of the word's letters. Lay the letters on your desk.

- Ask a classmate to put the letters in the correct order and use the word in a sentence.

Name_____

8. Farm Life

In Mrs. Brown Went to Town, the animals act more like people than animals. Choose one of the animals. Look up this animal in an encyclopedia. Make notes about

- how it lives
- what it eats
- what its job might be on a real farm

Use your notes to write a paragraph about the animal you chose. Draw a picture for your paragraph.

9. Story to Song!

Working in a small group, turn the story *Mrs. Brown Went to Town* into a song. Choose one of your favorite songs. Change the words so that they tell the story of Mrs. Brown and her animals. Practice your song.

10. Weather Reporter

Predict the weather for each day of the school week. Take a piece of drawing paper and divide it into five columns. Draw pictures to show your predictions. For example, if you predict that Monday will be sunny, draw a sun. Imagine that you are a weather reporter on television. Present your weather report to the class.

Name_____

1. The Big Dipper

In *Henry and Mudge and the Starry Night,* Henry and his family look up at the stars and see the Big Dipper and the Little Dipper. Make your own Big Dipper.

- On a piece of black construction paper, carefully sketch the outline of the Big Dipper.

- Make circles for each of the stars. Make the North Star circle bigger than the others.

- Using a pencil, carefully poke holes where you drew circles.

- Turn your paper over and hold it up to the light to see your Big Dipper.

2. Compound Match

Play this game with a classmate.

- Find and list five compound words from the *Henry and Mudge and the Starry Night.*

- Write each word on a strip of paper.

- Cut the word so that it makes its two smaller words.

- Mix up all the pieces. Lay all the smaller words on your desk, face up.

- Ask a classmate to connect the two smaller words to make a compound word.

3. My Favorite Place Outdoors

What is your favorite place outdoors? Is it a park? Is it the schoolyard?

Make a poster about this place.

- Draw a map or a picture of the place.
- Make a list of 10 reasons why this is your favorite place. For example: *I can play ball. There are lots of trees.*

Share your poster and list with a classmate.

4. Build a Tree House

Being in a tree house is one way to experience nature. You could sit in tree house and see amazing things.

- Draw a tree house.
- Imagine you are in the tree house. What would you do there? What would you see?
- Write a short story about it.
- Show your tree house and tell your story to the class.

5. My Outside Adventure

In *Henry and Mudge and the Starry Night*, Henry and Mudge go camping. Have you ever gone camping, on a picnic, or on an outdoor field trip? Write a story about a day you spent outside. Did you have fun? What did you like? What did you dislike? Be sure your story has a beginning, middle, and end. Draw a picture to go with your story. Share your story with a classmate.

Name_____

6. Postcard from the Outdoors

Imagine you have gone camping with your family in the woods, just like Henry and Mudge. Send a postcard to your class about your trip.

- Use an oaktag card to make your postcard. Draw a picture of something you saw while camping on one side of the card.

- Write a message to your class on the other side. In your message, explain the picture on the front side of the card.

- Sign your name after the message.

7. Nature Connections

Henry "ran like the wind" in the story *Henry and Mudge and the Starry Night.* What does it mean to "run like the wind"? Talk about it with a classmate. Then play Nature Connections.

- Write action words. For example: *sing, jump,* and *fall.*

- Invent phrases using the word *like.* The first word of the phrase must be an action word. The last word must be a word for something in nature. For example, *sing like a bird, jump like a kangaroo,* and *fall like rain.*

- Take turns with your classmate saying the phrases.

8. Campfire Categories

What kinds of things do you need on a camping trip? What kinds of things do you find when you get there? Make two webs, one for things you need and one for things you find. Use things from the story *Henry and Mudge and the Starry Night* to help you fill in your webs. Share your webs with a classmate.

9. From Here to There

Imagine you are taking a walk from your classroom to another place in your school.

- Choose a place where you want to go. Think of the best way to get there from your classroom.

- Draw a map of the path from your classroom to this place.

- Add words or pictures of things you see along the way.

Show and explain your map to the class.

10. National Parks

Henry and his family go camping. A popular place for people to camp is a National Park. The United States has several national parks all over the country. Use a Venn diagram like the one on page 71 of the Practice Book to compare and contrast two national parks in the United States. First, choose two national parks. You can look them up in an encyclopedia or on the national park website. Think about what is the same and what is different about the parks you choose. Use that information to complete the Venn diagram.

Name_____

1. What Am I Thinking Of?

In this game, your partner must guess what you are describing from a picture in *Exploring Parks with Ranger Dockett.*

- Choose a picture from the story.
- Choose an item in the picture to describe to your partner. Do not tell your partner what the item is.
- Using descriptive words, tell your partner about the item.
- See if you partner can guess the item.
- Switch roles and let your partner describe an item to you.

2. Park Statue

Look at the photographs of the different statues in Ranger Dockett's park. Make another statue for his park.

- Think about something that could be a statue.
- Draw a picture of your statue and paste your drawing to a piece of poster board.
- Write two or three sentences explaining why the statue would be a nice addition to the park. Write a sentence telling where in the park you would put the statue.

Theme Paperback

3. *Animal Tracks Are Everywhere/ Amelia Bedelia Goes Camping*

Read the story *Animal Tracks Are Everywhere* or *Amelia Bedelia Goes Camping.* Then fill in a story map using information from the story. Tell the story to a classmate in your own words, using the notes from your chart.

CM 2–5 Activity Master   Grade 2   Theme 2: Nature Walk

Name _____

4. Animal Squares

Play a game of animal squares with a classmate.

- Draw a large chart with five columns and five rows.

- At the top of each colum, write a letter of the alphabet.

- Fill in the rows with the names of animals that begin with each letter.

- Play again using different letters.

5. Park Adventures

Make up stories about adventures in a park with a small group of your classmates.

- One person in the group begins the story by naming a character and an event.

- Each member of the group adds one event to the story. All events must be about the character.

- The last person in the group must end the story.

- Then a different member of the group begins a new story. Everyone in the group should begin and end a new story.

6. Earth Day

Every year people all over the world celebrate Earth Day. On that day people do good things for nature. Make an Earth Day poster. Think of five things your class can do on Earth Day. Write them on the poster. Add drawings and photographs. Give your poster a title. Display your poster and read your ideas to a classmate.

Name _____

7. Pet Survey

Do your classmates have pets? What kind are they? First, take a survey. Ask your classmates the question: *What kind of pet do you have?* Write the answer into your notebook. If a classmate doesn't have a pet, write *none*. If a classmate has more than one pet, find out about all of them. Make a graphic like the one shown to show the results of your survey. Share your findings with the class.

Dog	✓ ✓ ✓ ✓ ✓
Cat	✓ ✓ ✓
Fish	✓ ✓ ✓ ✓ ✓ ✓
Snake	✓

8. My Garden

A garden is like a small park. Design your own garden. Make a card for each thing you want in your garden.

- Draw a flower or vegetable that you want. Write its name if you can.

- Make 12 cards.

- Spread the cards out on your table. Decide where you would like to put each thing in the garden.

- Arrange the cards to make a garden design.

- Then glue the cards in that order to a big piece of paper. Draw different animals or a path around your garden.

Ask a classmate to look at your garden. Tell about it.

9. Park Poem

Write a poem about taking a walk in Ranger Dockett's park.

- Reread *Exploring Parks with Ranger Dockett.* Make notes about the things you see.

- Write a poem. You can use a complete sentence or parts of a sentence for each line.

- If you want, you can make some of the words rhyme.

- Use words that tell about what happens during your walk. Describe colors, sights, sounds, smells, and feelings.

Read your poem to the class.

10. Fact or Opinion?

- Choose an animal or plant that you might find in Ranger Dockett's park.

- Using a K-W-L chart, write down things you know about that animal in the first column.

- In the second column, write questions about what you want to know about that animal.

- Read about your animal. Find the answers to your questions.

- Write what you learn in the last column.

- Review your chart and write *F* next to things in the first column that you proved were facts. If anything you read was someone's opinion, write *O* next to it.

Name_____

1. Colorful Words

The children pick blueberries in the story *Around the Pond: Who's Been Here?* The word *blueberry* is a compound word. It is made up of two words: *blue* and *berry*. How many compound words with colors do you know?

- Make a chart with six columns.

- Label the columns: *black*, *blue*, *red*, and *white*. Add two more colors to your chart.

- Write compound words that you already know.

- Look up more words in a dictionary. Complete your chart with as many colorful words as you can.

Make up sentences with a classmate. Use each of your compound words in a sentence.

2. Animal Descriptions

Play this animal game with a classmate.

- Write words that describe how animals look. For example: *tail*, *fur*, and *claws*.

- Choose words from the list and write one word on each card. Make at least six cards.

- Divide the cards between you and your classmate.

- On the back of the card, write the names of animals that fit the category on the front of the card.

Look over the completed cards. Talk about how the animals are the same or different.

Name _____

3. Wow!

You have learned that an exclamation is a sentence that shows strong feeling, such as surprise or fear. It ends with an exclamation point. Look at the pictures of the animals in *Around the Pond: Who's Been There?* Write two exclamation sentences or words for each animal picture. For example: *What a long neck! Look at the bright colors!*

Show the picture of the animal and read your exclamations to the class.

4. Nature Puzzle

A picture puzzle is a picture that is cut up into pieces. Make a puzzle and see if a classmate can solve it.

- Paint that scene on a piece of drawing paper. Include details, such as animals and plants.

- Be sure your scene is clearly drawn so that when you cut it, you can remember how it should look.

- Let the picture dry. Fold the paper four times. Cut the picture into squares along the folds.

- Mix the squares up. These are your puzzle pieces.

Give the squares to classmates. Can they solve the puzzle?

5. Life Cycles

Choose an animal from *Around the Pond: Who's Been Here?* and find the steps in its life cycle. Use what you learn to make a diagram that shows its life cycle.

6. Wildlife Collage

Cammy and William see all kinds of wildlife. Make a collage of different kinds of animals and plants that live around lakes and ponds. Use pictures from old magazines. Share your collage with a classmate.

7. Naturalists

Naturalists are people who love nature. One famous naturalist was John Muir. Find out about John Muir and write a short report. In your report include information about his life and the important things he has done to help nature. Include a drawing or photograph of John Muir.

8. What Do You See?

Cammy and William use clues to identify animals that live by the pond. You can use clues to help some classmates identify things in the classroom.

- Choose an object in the classroom, but do not tell anyone what it is.

- Give one descriptive clue at a time about the object until someone guesses what it is.

Try not to look at the object when you give the clues. A classmate might guess the object by noticing where you are looking!

Name_____

9. Thumbprint Detective

Like the animals in *Around the Pond: Who's Been Here?*, people have special prints—fingerprints! Be a detective and match thumbprints to the person they belong to!

- Fold and index card in half. Press your thumb into a stamp pad.

- Slowly and carefully stamp your inked thumb on one half of the index card. Repeat the print for the other half of the card. Be sure to use the same thumb on each half.

- Clean the ink off your thumb. Cut your card on the fold. Write your name on the back of each half.

- Get together with other classmates who have cards. Each person puts one of their two cards on a table, thumbprint side up. Put all the other cards in a pile and shuffle them. Lay the pile thumbprint side up.

- Each person picks a card from the pile. All together, try and match the card you chose to one laying on the table.

10. Puppet Show

Create and present a puppet show with your classmates. Draw, color, and cut animals from the selection out of paper. Tape the paper animals to craft sticks. Imagine what the animals think and do when they see the children and their dog. Act out the story, using your puppets.

Name_____

1. New Year Resolutions

The start of a new year is a time when people make *resolutions,* or decisions to make changes in their lives. Make your own list of resolutions. Think about

- new activities you want to try

- new ways to act and do things

Write ten resolutions and number them. For example:

1. *I will read more books.*

2. *I will be nicer to my brother.*

Read and explain your list to a classmate.

Phonics
Library

2. *Mother's Day Parade on Park Street*

Reread the story *Mother's Day Parade on Park Street.* Then make a chart to tell what you liked and what you didn't like about the story. Your chart should look like this:

What I Liked	What I Didn't Like	Reasons Why I Feel This Way

With a classmate, talk about the things listed in your chart.

Name_____

3. Paper Bag Story

Create a surprise story about things in your neighborhood.

- Tear or cut 12 strips of paper. Write one word on each strip.

- Six of the words must name a place, person, or thing in your neighborhood.

- Six of the words must be action verbs.

Get together with classmates. Put your words into a paper bag. Follow these steps to tell a story:

- Take one strip of paper out of the bag at a time.

- Use the word in a sentence to begin the story. Don't put the strip of paper back in the bag.

- The next person continues the story by picking a word out of the bag and using it in a sentence.

- Continue the story until there are no more strips of paper.

4. Neighborhood Flag

Make a flag for your neighborhood to display during an important celebration.

- Use colors that tell about your neighborhood. For example, green might show that there are lots of trees.

- Use shapes or objects that you see in your neighborhood. For example, draw a sun if it's usually sunny or draw a special bird that lives there.

Draw the flag and show it to a classmate. Explain the colors, shapes, and objects.

Name_____

5. What Happens Next?

What did the boy do after he finished shopping in *Chinatown?* The author doesn't tell us.

Look at the pictures on pages 234–249. Imagine what the boy does after that. Write a story about what happens. Write at least 12 sentences.

Compare your story with a classmate's story. Did you imagine the same events as your classmate?

6. Fun in the Neighborhood

Plan a special event for your neighborhood. Think about the best time of year for the event. What can everyone do together during this time of the year? Make a list of different events. Write a paragraph about the event you chose. Compare your idea with a classmate's idea. What is alike or different about them?

7. Plan a Parade

You are in charge of planning a neighborhood parade. Draw a map of your neighborhood. Show and label streets and buildings on the map. Look at your map and think about where the parade will start and end. Plan the best way for the parade to go from start to finish. Show the map to a classmate and describe your plan.

Name _____

8. My Favorite Place

What is your favorite place in your town or city? Make a poster about your favorite place.

- Draw a picture of your favorite place at the top.
- Write at least three sentences to describe the place.
- Write a title for your poster.

Share the poster with a classmate.

9. Hopscotch

Hopscotch is a neighborhood game that brings children of a community together. Make your own hopscotch diagram.

- Use any shapes that you like in the diagram.
- Write numbers in the shapes where you can land.
- Don't put numbers on the shapes that you skip over.

Show your hopscotch diagram to a classmate.

10. Card for My Neighborhood

Make a card for the people in your neighborhood.

- Fold a sheet of paper into the shape of a card.
- On the cover of the card, draw a picture of something in your neighborhood.
- Write a poem about your neighborhood inside the card.
- Don't forget to sign your name.

Share your card with a group of classmates.

Name_____

1. Pretend Pets

Spot is the name of the pet dog in *A Trip to the Firehouse.*
Why is Spot a good name? Think of an animal you would
like as a pet. What name would you give it and why?

- Draw a picture of your favorite kind of animal.

- Give your pretend pet a name.

- Write the main idea and details
  that tell why the name is a good
  one for your pretend pet. For
  example: *Main Idea: Scruffy is a
  good name for my pet. Details:
  He has a lot of fur. The fur is always a mess.*

Tell a classmate about your pretend pet and its name.

2. Firefighter Interview

In the story you learn a lot about the jobs of firefighters.
With a partner, act out an interview. Each of you should
prepare questions you would like to ask a firefighter. Then,
one of you plays the interviewer and one of you plays the
firefighter. Switch roles and interview again.

On My
Way
Practice
Reader

Theme
Paperback

3. *Catching Bailey/Harry's Pony*

Read the story *Catching Bailey* or *Harry's Pony.* Use a story
map to show the characters, setting, and events at the
beginning, middle, and end of the story. Share your map
with a classmate who read the same story. Talk about what
happened in the story.

Name_____

4. Bicycle Checklist

Reread pages 283–286 of *A Trip to the Firehouse,* which tell how firefighters keep everything in perfect working order. Write a checklist.

- List these parts of a bicycle: *tires, handlebars, brakes, seat, pedals, chain, reflector, light,* and *bell or horn.* Look up any words you don't know in a dictionary.

- Think about what you need to do to keep a bicycle in good working order.

- Write a step on your checklist for each bicycle part.

Read your checklist to a classmate.

5. Helmet

Firefighters wear helmets. Who else wears helmets? Use a word web to answer this question. In the center circle, write the word *Helmets.* In the other circles, write other jobs or sports that use helmets. Share your web with a classmate.

6. Compounds

Play this game with a partner.

- Write each of the words on page 159 of the Practice Book on a separate index card. Then write each of these words on a separate index card: *up, side, house, stairs, in,* and *fire.*

- Lay all the cards face down on a desk. Player 1 turns over two cards. If the words make a compound word, player 1 gets to keep the cards. If not, it is player 2's turn.

Name_____

7. Uniforms

Like firefighters, other people wear uniforms at work. For example: *crossing guard, police officer, nurse, mail carrier,* or *pilot.* Choose your favorite uniform.

- Draw a picture of a person wearing the uniform.

- Write about the person's job.

Show your picture to a classmate. Read the job description. Tell why the job is important.

8. Dial a Number

If you need help from people in your community, such as firefighters, you can call them with a telephone. With a classmate, make a telephone keypad.

- Use a large index card or cut a big rectangle from stiff paper.

- Divide the rectangle into 12 squares, like a telephone keypad.

- Then write in the numbers and symbols.

- One person reads phone numbers from the list of important numbers in Rosewood City.

- The other person dials the numbers on the keypad. Switch roles and dial again.

Name_____

9. Firehouse Noises

Firehouses are noisy places. What makes the sounds?

- Make a chart with two columns. Label one column *Sound Maker* and the other *Sound.*

- Find things that make noises in *A Trip to the Firehouse.* Write them in the first column. For example: *bell.*

- Then describes the sound each thing makes. Write the sounds in the second column. For example: *clang.*

Read the words in your chart to a classmate. Try to imitate the sounds.

10. Fire Trucks

On pages 280–281 of *A Trip to the Firehouse,* there are pictures of five different kinds of fire trucks. With a partner, find out which of these trucks are used at your local fire station. Make a poster that shows

- the name of your local fire station

- pictures of the trucks used there and their names

Name_____

1. Picture Search

Look carefully at the picture on the cover of *Big Bushy Mustache.* What is different about Ricky and his father?

- Examine colors, shapes, faces, clothes, and other features.

- Write at least seven things that are different.

Compare your list with a classmate's. Did your classmate see other things that are different? Talk about how Ricky and his father are different.

2. Who Am I?

If you could be someone else, who would you be? Make your own costume.

- Look at "Costumes and Disguises" on pages 296–297.

- Think about the different costumes you can make.

- Use construction paper and decorate your own costume.

Show your costume to a classmate. Have him or her guess who you are pretending to be and then tell why you chose your costume.

3. What If?

What if Ricky's dad didn't have a mustache to give him? What could Ricky do to solve his problem? Read pages 318–319 of *Big Bushy Mustache.* Make a list of the things that Ricky tried. Can you come up with different solutions? Write them down.

Name_____

4. Spanish Glossary

Make a glossary of the Spanish words in *Big Bushy Mustache.*

- Find and list all the Spanish words in *Big Bushy Mustache.*

- Write a definition for each word on your list. Use a Spanish-English dictionary to help you.

Compare your glossary to a classmate's. Did you come up with the same definitions?

5. What Would He Say?

What do you think Ricky would say to his friends about where he got his new mustache? Write a dialogue between Ricky and one of his friends. Tell how Ricky lost his mustache and how his father helped him. Have the friend respond and ask questions about his story. Use the dialogue in the selection as a model. Be sure to use quotation marks before and after spoken words. Act out your dialogue with a classmate.

6. Ricky's Answers

Ricky meets three people on the street. Look at pages 308–309 of the story to find out about them.

- Think about what each person says or does. Should Ricky answer them in words, actions, or both?

- Write Ricky's response to these people.

Act out your responses with a classmate.

Name_____

7. Language Survey
Find out how many languages your classmates speak. Conduct a survey.

- Make a chart with three columns like the one below.

- Ask classmates, *What languages do you speak?*

- Write the name of the language in the first column.

- Write the name of the person who speaks the language in the second column.

- Add up the names in the second column. Write the total number in the last column.

Share your results with the class.

Language	Speakers	Total

8. *¡Gracias, papá!*
In the story, Ricky's father shaves off his mustache so that Ricky can use it in the play. Make a thank-you card that Ricky might have made for his father. Title your card *¡Gracias, papá!*, which is Spanish for *Thank you, Father!* Draw pictures and designs and write a short message.

9. Meaning Match

Play this matching game with a classmate.

- Find a list of the words on pages 178–179 of the Practice Book.

- Write each word on an index card. Write each meaning on a separate index card.

- Lay all the meanings face-up on your desk. Put all the words in a card pile face down.

- Player 1 chooses a word from the card pile and tries to match the word to its meaning. If player 1 makes a match, he or she keeps the cards. If not, it is the next player's turn.

- Play continues until all cards have been matched.

10. Calendar Quiz

Work with a partner to answer the following questions. Use a year-long calendar to help you.

- Which month has the least number of days?

- What day of the week does your birthday fall on?

- What months do you go to school?

JANUARY	FEBRUARY	MARCH	APRIL	MAY	JUNE
M T W T F S S	M T W T F S S	M T W T F S S	M T W T F S S	M T W T F S S	M T W T F S S
1 2 3 4 5 6 7	1 2 3 4	1 2 3 4	1	1 2 3 4 5 6	1 2 3
8 9 10 11 12 13 14	5 6 7 8 9 10 11	5 6 7 8 9 10 11	2 3 4 5 6 7 8	7 8 9 10 11 12 13	4 5 6 7 8 9 10
15 16 17 18 19 20 21	12 13 14 15 16 17 18	12 13 14 15 16 17 18	9 10 11 12 13 14 15	14 15 16 17 18 19 20	11 12 13 14 15 16 17
22 23 24 25 26 27 28	19 20 21 22 23 24 25	19 20 21 22 23 24 25	16 17 18 19 20 21 22	21 22 23 24 25 26 27	18 19 20 21 22 23 24
29 30 31	26 27 28	26 27 28 29 30 31	23 24 25 26 27 28 29 30	28 29 30 31	25 26 27 28 29 30

JULY	AUGUST	SEPTEMBER	OCTOBER	NOVEMBER	DECEMBER
M T W T F S S	M T W T F S S	M T W T F S S	M T W T F S S	M T W T F S S	M T W T F S S
1	1 2 3 4 5	1 2	1 2 3 4 5 6 7	1 2 3 4	1 2
2 3 4 5 6 7 8	6 7 8 9 10 11 12	3 4 5 6 7 8 9	8 9 10 11 12 13 14	5 6 7 8 9 10 11	3 4 5 6 7 8 9
9 10 11 12 13 14 15	13 14 15 16 17 18 19	10 11 12 13 14 15 16	15 16 17 18 19 20 21	12 13 14 15 16 17 18	10 11 12 13 14 15 16
16 17 18 19 20 21 22	20 21 22 23 24 25 26	17 18 19 20 21 22 23	22 23 24 25 26 27 28	19 20 21 22 23 24 25	17 18 19 20 21 22 23
23 24 25 26 27 28 29	27 28 29 30 31	24 25 26 27 28 29 30	29 30 31	26 27 28 29 30	24 25 26 27 28 29 30
30 31					31

Name _____

1. My Detailed Day

In the story *Jamaica Louise James,* Grammy tells Jamaica about all the interesting people she sees on the subway. Think about all the people and things you see each day. Write a short story that describes a day in your life. In your story use

- descriptive words
- sensory details

2. Transportation

In *Jamaica Louise James,* Grammy rides the subway everyday. The subway is one kind of transportation. Divide a sheet of drawing paper into four sections. Think of four other kinds of transportation that people use. Draw a picture of each kind of transportation in the sections, one for each section. Share your drawings with a classmate.

3. Birthday Gift

In the selection, *Jamaica Louise James,* Jamaica got a paint set for her birthday. What do you want for your birthday?

- Write the name of the gift you want.
- Write a paragraph telling why you want it.
- Draw a picture of the gift.

4. Word Scramble

Make a list of all the vocabulary words from *Jamaica Louise James* on page 197 of the Practice Book.

- Under each word scramble the letters to make a scrambled word. For example, BOOTH could become TOBHO.

- Copy your scrambles on to another sheet of paper and ask a classmate to unscramble them.

- Check to see if he or she unscrambled the words correctly.

- Then have the classmate use the word in a sentence.

5. *Catching Bailey*

Play this yes or no question game with a classmate. Use the story *Catching Bailey* to help you.

- Each player writes three questions about the story to which the answer is yes.

- Each player writes three questions about the story to which the answer is no.

- Write each question on the front of an index card. On the back, write *yes* or *no.*

- Mix up the cards. Choose a card from your pile and read the question to a classmate.

- Ask the classmate to answer *yes* or *no.* If the answer is no, ask the classmate to explain why.

- Take turns asking and answering questions.

6. Tell Me Why

Play this guessing game with a classmate. Go to page 345 in *Jamaica Louise James.* Look at Jamaica's drawing.

- Think about what is happening in her drawing.

- Write questions about the drawing beginning with *Why.* Write at least five questions. For example: *Why is the woman wearing cowboy boots?*

Ask your classmate to use his or her imagination to guess the answer to your questions. Remember there are no wrong answers.

7. Famous Artists

In *Jamaica Louise James*, Jamaica wants to be an artist. Find out about a famous artist who interests you. Then write a report on his or her life. In your report, include

- when the artist was born

- where the artist lived

- interesting information on his or her life

- names of famous paintings, sculptures, or drawings

Name _____

8. Subway Art

Imagine that you are one of the people who rode the subway the day Jamaica put up all her pictures. Write a journal entry that you might have written after seeing her pictures. In your entry, describe the pictures and how they made you feel.

9. Character Descriptions

Choose a character from any of the selections in *Theme 3: Around Town: Neighborhood and Community*. Make a web for the character. Put the character's name in the center circle. In the other circles, write words that describe the character. Compare your web with a classmate who chose the same character. Add any new words to your web.

10. Guide Me

- Working with a partner, choose ten spelling words from the list on page 245 of the Practice Book.

- List them on a sheet of paper in alphabetical order.

- Look up each word in a dictionary.

- Write the guide words you find at the top of the dictionary page for that word next to the word.

Name_____

1. You're Invited

Make an invitation asking Officer Buckle and Gloria to come to your school. Be sure your invitation has the following information:

- whom the invitation is for

- why you are inviting them

- what time to come

- where they are to go once they arrive

- whom the invitation is from

Decorate your invitation. Read it to a classmate.

2. Oscar's Events

- Make a numbered list of events from *Oscar's Enormous Purr* in the order that they happened.

- Write each event on a separate index card. On the back of the card, write the number.

- Mix the cards up and place them event-side up.

- Ask a classmate to reorder the cards. Turn them over to see if he or she is correct.

Name _____

3. Crossing the Road

In *Officer Buckle and Gloria,* Officer Buckle lists all kinds of safety tips. What safety tips do you follow when you cross a road? Think about

- what you do before you cross and how you walk across

- obeying traffic signs and lights

Draw some safety tips and make a poster.

4. Good Dog

Commanding is a way to tell a dog to do a trick.

- Look at pictures in *Officer Buckle and Gloria* that show what Gloria is doing while Officer Buckle is talking.

- Write a command for each of Gloria's actions and the page number the picture is on. For example: *Point your finger, Gloria. Page 26.*

Share your commands with a classmate.

5. Missing Words

- Choose five safety tips Officer Buckle shared.

- Write each tip, leaving out one of the important words. Replace that word with a blank. For example: *Keep your _____ tied.*

- Give your safety tips to a classmate. Ask your classmate to write the missing words.

Name_____

6. Noise Words

   Look at page 46 in *Officer Buckle and Gloria*. There are
four words that sound like a noise: *splat*, *splatter*, *sploosh*,
and *smack*.

- Think of four more words that sound like a noise.

- Use each of your noise words in a sentence.

- Share your sentences with a classmate.

7. News Hound

   Sometimes a reporter is called a *news hound*. This is
because he or she "sniffs" out a story. Imagine you are
a news hound. Write a short news story about what
happened on page 46 and 47 of *Officer Buckle and Gloria*.

- Make notes of all the details from the pictures.

- Think of *Who? What? Where? When? How?* and *Why?*
  when you write.

- Make your story as descriptive as possible.

- Practice reading your news story.

8. What's Next?

   Can you predict the outcome of *Officer Buckle and Gloria?*
Do you think they will stay partners or break up? Support
your prediction with details from the story.

Name_____

9. Guess Who?

Play a guessing game with a partner.

- Find five sentences in *Officer Buckle and Gloria* that have a character's name in them.

- Change the name to a pronoun, such as *she* or *he*. Rewrite the sentences with pronouns in place of the name. For example: "Officer Buckle was shocked" would become "He was shocked."

- Exchange your sentences with your partner. See if your partner can guess who the pronoun replaced.

10. Animal Match

Play this matching game with a classmate.

- Make a list of six animals.

- Find out what the babies of the animals are called.

- Place each name of the parents and babies on a separate index card.

- Mix up the cards. Lay all the index cards face down

- The first player turns over two cards and tries to match a parent with its baby.

- If a match is made, the player keeps the cards. If not, the cards get turned back over and it is the next player's turn.

- Play continues until all matches are made.

Name _____

1. Cooperation

Ants cooperate. *Cooperation* means working together. Divide a sheet of paper into two columns.

- In the first column, write five ways that ants cooperate in the story *Ant*.

- Compare the five ways to how people cooperate. Write your ideas in the second column. For example: *Ants feed their babies and each other. People feed their babies.*

Share your chart with a classmate.

2. Giant Pandas

In the story *Hank's Pandas,* Hank works with giant pandas at a zoo. The National Zoo in Washington, D.C. has two giant pandas that were given to the United States by China. Find out about these pandas in an encyclopedia or on the Internet. Write a paragraph about what you learn. Draw a picture to go with your paragraph.

3. Ant Picnic

The ants from the story *Ant* are having a picnic.

- Find each kind of ants' favorite food in *Ant*.

- Make a picnic announcement. Write the menu on it. Be sure to include at least one food for each kind of ant.

- Decorate the announcement.

4. Match the Ants

Create a matching game. You need index cards.

- Make a list of all the kinds of ants in the story *Ant.*

- Write two details about each kind of ant next to its name.

- Write the name of each ant on one index card and its two details on another.

- Lay all the cards face down on your desk.

- The first player turns over two cards, trying to match the ant with its details. If they match, the player keeps the match. If not, the player turns the cards over and it is the next player's turn.

5. Insect Poetry

Write a counting poem about insects.

- Each line of the poem must begin with a number and the name of an insect. For example: *Three flies sat on a tree.* Try to use a different insect for each line.

- Start the poem with number one and continue to number ten.

- Draw a picture to go with your poem.

- Read your poem to a classmate.

6. Ant Maze

Draw an ant maze on a piece of drawing paper. Use examples of mazes to help you.

- Draw a line at the top of the page to show the ground level. Leave an opening. Label it *Enter.*

- Draw a path from the opening to the bottom right corner of the paper. Label this *Home.*

- Make lots of twists and turns in your main path.

- Add sections off the main path that lead to dead ends.

Ask a classmate to solve the maze.

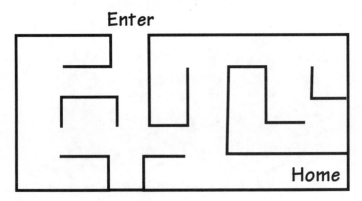

Enter

Home

7. Fun Fact Poster

Choose one of the kinds of ants mentioned in *Ant.* Make a fun fact poster about that ant.

- Go to pages 58–59 in the story, *Ant.* You will see examples of fun facts.

- Find two fun facts about the ant you chose.

- Write the fun facts on your poster.

- Add drawings of the ant to your poster.

Share your poster with the class. Explain the fun facts.

Grade 2   Theme 4: Amazing Animals

8. Human Antennae

In the selection *Ants*, you learn that ants have antennae that act like "a nose and fingers all in one." Ants identify things with their antennae. Can you use your fingers to do the same?

- Collect eight small objects. Put the objects in a bag or small box with a lid. Don't let anyone see what you are collecting.

- Ask a classmate to close his or her eyes. Give your classmate an object from the bag.

- Tell the classmate to guess what it is by touching it.

9. *Raptors*

Read the book *Raptors.* As you read, think about what happens in the book. Use a noting details chart to write three questions about the story.

- Write the answer to each question.

- Quiz a classmate who read the same book. Ask the classmate to answer your questions. Give clues if the classmate isn't sure about an answer.

10. *Sandy Goes to the Vet*

Read the story, *Sandy Goes to the Vet.* Fill in a story map about the story. Include characters, setting, and events that happened at the beginning, middle, and end of the story.

Use your map to retell the story to a classmate.

Name_____

1. Teamwork

In *The Great Ball Game,* the members of each team contribute different skills to the game. Pick new animals to be on the "teeth" team and list their skills.

- Divide a sheet of paper in half. Label one half *column 1* and the other half *column 2.*

- In column 1, list six new animals for the "teeth" team.

- In column 2, write notes about each new team member's skill and why he or she is good for the team. For example: *A giraffe has a long neck and runs fast.*

- Draw your favorite new team member.

Read and explain your choices to a classmate.

Phonics Library

2. *Crow's Plan*

Reread the story *Crow's Plan.* What is the problem that the animals try to solve? How do they solve it? Use a problem/solution chart to show what happens in the story. Share your chart with a classmate.

3. Animal Homes

Choose an animal from *The Great Ball Game* and one other animal that interests you. Where do these animals live? Find out about each of the animal's homes in the encyclopedia or other books. Make notes about where it lives or builds its home. Then use a Venn diagram to compare and contrast the two animals' homes.

4. Animal Charades

Play animal charades with some classmates.

- Make a word card for each animal in *The Great Ball Game.*

- Shuffle the cards and place them face down.

- Choose a card and look at the name. Keep it a secret.

- Act like the animal without using words. Ask your classmates to guess what animal you are.

- For each guess, say *yes* or *no.* Do not give hints.

Take turns playing until all the cards are played.

5. Story Dictionary

Make a list of five words from the story that a reader might need help with. Put the words in alphabetical order. Make a dictionary entry for each word. Be sure that

- each word has a meaning and a sample sentence

- if possible, each word has a picture

Use your glossary to remind you how to write a dictionary entry. Use a dictionary to help you with meanings. Do not pick words that are already in your glossary.

Name_____

6. Name That Team!

The teams in *The Great Ball Game* each need a team name.

• Think of a good name for one of the teams in the story.

• Think of an interesting badge for the team uniforms. Draw one and cut it out.

• Be sure to write the team name on the badge.

Show your badge to the class. Explain why you picked the name you did.

7. Animal Fables

The story *The Great Ball Game* is a fable. *Fables* are stories that try to explain why something happens, or they can teach a lesson. The story *The Great Ball Game* explains why birds fly south for the winter.

• Read one of Aesop's animal fables or another well-known fable.

• Write down what you think the fable is explaining or the lesson it is teaching.

• Tell the fable to a classmate. Ask him or her to tell you what it is explaining or teaching and see if your answers match.

Name_____

8. Artist

Get together with a classmate and look at the illustrations in *The Great Ball Game.* Talk about the materials the artist used. Make a picture of your favorite sport using different materials like the pictures in the story. Some materials you might use: *construction paper, cotton, felt, thread, buttons,* and *wallpaper scraps.*

9. Sticky Situation

In *The Great Ball Game,* the animal team wins the game because of the bat. How would the outcome of the story change if the bird team had chosen the bat instead? Write a new ending to the story.

10. News Article

Imagine that you are a reporter and you have been asked to write an article about the big game and its outcome in *The Great Ball Game.* When writing your article think about *Who? What? When? Where? Why?* and *How?* Be sure to include

- a headline that makes the reader want to know more
- an exciting topic sentence
- important facts and details about the events

Name _____

1. You're the Teacher

Imagine there's a new baby in your house. What can you teach the baby?

- Write four things you can teach.

- How would you teach these things? Give lots of details.

Read your ideas to a classmate. Tell why it would be fun.

Phonics Library

2. *My Sister Joan*

In the story, *My Sister Joan,* Kevin has the nickname *Buster.* Do you have a nickname? If so, use it for this activity. If not, make up a nickname for yourself. Write a paragraph that tells about your nickname. Tell what it is, where it came from or why you chose it, and why it is special to you. Tell a classmate about your nickname and why it is special.

3. Privacy Rules

Everyone needs privacy sometimes. *Privacy* means your own space or quiet time. Make up privacy rules. Write a list telling others what to do or not to do to give people some privacy. Read your list to a family member at home. Talk with them about why privacy is important in a family.

4. Tell About Twins

Look at the pictures on page 135 in *Brothers and Sisters.* Read about the twins. Make a web about what is the same about twins. Include many details on your web. Show your web to a classmate, and ask if he or she can think of anything to add. Talk about whether it would be fun to be a twin.

5. Toy Inventor

Babies love toys. Invent a new toy for a baby.

- Think about a toy that is safe and fun for a baby.

- Draw your invention. Label the parts of the toy.

- Write a paragraph about your toy. Tell how the toy works and why it is fun to play with.

Show your new toy to a classmate and explain how it works.

6. Younger Children

What are most younger children like?

- Divide a piece of paper in half.

- In the first column, write three generalizations about younger children.

- In the second column, write supporting examples for each generalization.

Compare your chart with a classmate's. Did you have the same ideas?

Name_____

7. Brother, Sister Survey

Who has brothers or sisters in your class? Conduct a survey.

- Make a chart like the one below. Write names of classmates in the first column.

- Then ask classmates these two questions: *How many brothers do you have? How many sisters do you have?*

- Write the answers in the chart. If your classmates don't have brothers or sisters, write *0.*

- Add up the numbers in the columns.

Present the results of your survey to classmates.

Name	Brothers	Sisters

8. Make the Connection

Play this word game with a classmate.

- First, make 10 word cards with people's names.

- Shuffle the cards and put them face down between you.

- Each player takes a card from the top of the stack.

- Invent family connections to go with the names. For example: *Card #1: Jason, Card #2: Sara, Connection: Sara is Jason's aunt.*

Once you finish, draw a picture of the family you made.

Name_____

9. Family Poetry

Reread the poems in "Brother and Sister Poems" on pages 148–151 of your book. Write a poem about anyone in your family. Your poem can

- rhyme

- have short or long lines

- be serious or funny

Draw a picture to go with your poem.

10. You're Special!

Show a family member that you appreciate him or her. Create an "I Think You're Special" card.

- Choose a family member for the card.

- Fold a sheet of paper to make the card. Draw a picture on the cover.

- Write a greeting on the cover with the person's name.

- Write a four-line message or poem inside the card.

Read your poem to a classmate.

Name _____

Phonics Library

1. *Lost and Found*

Reread the story *Lost and Found* and fill in a story map showing what happens in the story. Be sure to include

- setting

- characters

- events in the beginning, middle, and end

Use your story map to retell the story to the class.

2. My Bagel

In the story, the father liked lox on his bagel. What do you like on your bagel? Draw a picture of a bagel and your favorite topping. Write a few sentences about what you like to put on a bagel. Show your picture to a classmate and tell about your bagel.

3. Trip to Israel

Make a travel poster for Israel.

- Look up facts about Israel in an encyclopedia.

- Write at least one interesting fact about this country.

- Write about one feature that you think people should see.

Display your poster on a bulletin board.

Name _____

Theme
Paperback

4. *Swim Dad!/Tonight is Carnaval*

Reread the story *Swim, Dad!* or *Tonight is Carnaval.*

- Choose one activity done by any of the characters.
- Write directions that tell how to do the activity.
- Write all the steps in order.

Read the directions to a classmate. Have him or her ask you any questions about the activity.

5. Hot, Hot Jalapeño!

Jalapeños belong to the vegetable group called *peppers.* Make a jalapeño fact file.

- Find out about jalapeños in an encyclopedia.
- Write facts about this pepper on an index card.
- Draw a jalapeño on the card.

Take your card home to share with a family member. Think of a way you can use jalapeños in a recipe.

6. At the Bakery

What do bakers bake in a bakery?

- Fill in a word web about bakery foods.
- Brainstorm all the baked foods you've tried or would like to try.
- Show the web to a classmate. Discuss your favorite baked foods.

Name _____

7. Dream Ice Cream

Invent an ice-cream dish. Make a recipe card for this great dessert.

- Write the ice-cream flavors.
- Write the toppings.
- Write measurements for each ingredient.

Share your recipe with a family member and see if he or she can follow your directions to make your dessert.

8. Favorite Flavor Survey

What is everyone's favorite ice-cream flavor? Conduct a survey.

- Make a chart with two columns like the one below. Label the columns *Name* and *Flavor.*
- Write names of classmates in the first column.
- Then ask classmates the question: *What is your favorite ice-cream flavor?*
- Write the answers in the chart.

Make a graph to display your results.

Name	Flavor

Grade 2   Theme 5: Family Time

9. International Bagels

In the story, Mexican jalapeños were added to Jewish bagels. Invent bagels with other international flavors.

- Think of foods popular in other cultures. For example: *Italian pepperoni.*

- Find more ideas in an encyclopedia. Look up different countries.

Make three different bagels from craft dough.

- Follow the directions on page 166 in *Jalapeño Bagels.*

- Add different colors of craft dough for special ingredients.

- Give your bagels a name. For example: *pepperoni bagel.*

Show your bagels in a small group. Explain why you chose your ingredients.

10. Food Safety

Reread the safety tips for cooking on page 181 of your book. Choose three tips and make a poster that shows the tips your chose. Write out each tip and draw a picture that shows the meaning of the tip. Share your posters with the class.

Name _____

1. *Aunt Lizzie Finds Her Cake*

In the story *Aunt Lizzie Finds Her Cake,* Willy and Pam place clues all over the house to help Aunt Lizzie find her cake.

- Draw and cut out a picture of a cake.

- Hide your cake somewhere in the classroom.

- Write four clues like the clues in the story to help a classmate find your cake. Each clue should lead to another clue and the fourth clue should lead to the cake.

- Place the clues in their proper hiding place.

- Give the first clue to a classmate and see if he or she can find your hidden cake.

2. Fun Fair!

Make a web about a fair.

- What are some activities at a fair? Brainstorm ideas and write them in the web. For example: *rides, food.*

- Expand the web to give specific details. For example: *Ferris wheel, popcorn.*

Talk to a classmate about what you can do at a fair.

Name_____

3. Your Favorite Gift

In the story *Carousel*, Alex gets a miniature carousel for her birthday. Think about a favorite gift that you got for your birthday. Draw a picture of the gift and write a paragraph under the picture that tells

- what it is and who gave it to you

- why it is your favorite gift

Share your pictures with a classmate.

4. Spelling Game

Play this spelling game with a classmate.

- Write each of the spelling words found on page 237 of the Practice Book on separate index cards.

- Place all the cards, face down, in a pile.

- Player 1 chooses a card and tells player 2 the word. Player 2 must then spell the word. If player 2 spells it correctly, he or she keeps the card. If not, the card goes back in the pile.

- Then player 2 picks a card and asks player 1 to spell it.

- Play continues until all the cards have been used.

5. Thank You!

Alex did not thank her family and friends for the gifts she got. Write a thank-you note that Alex should have written to her family and friends. Be sure to say thank you for the gifts she got and why she liked them.

Name _____

6. You're Invited!

Make an invitation to a party with a fair theme.

- Fold a sheet of construction paper in half to make a card.

- Draw a picture on the cover. Show one of the fun games or rides at the party.

Write details about the party inside the invitation. Include the following:

- the reason for the party, such as a birthday or summer vacation

- the date and time of the party

- the location

Pass your invitation around for classmates to read. Describe what special attractions and games will be at the party.

7. Carousel Critter

What animal would you like to see on a carousel? Design a new carousel critter. Use your imagination. Draw a picture of your new carousel critter. Write under the picture why you chose that critter and why you think it would be a good addition to a carousel. Share your drawing and ideas with the class.

8. Alex's Carousel

Write an information paragraph about Alex's carousel.

- Begin with a topic sentence that tells what the paragraph is about. Indent the first word.

- Then write four sentences about the topic.

- Look at a picture of Alex's carousel to remember details.

Read your paragraph to a classmate.

9. Wild Safari

Imagine that a carousel company wants you to go on an African safari. Your job is to observe animals that would be good for their new African carousel. Look for animals only found in Africa. Use an encyclopedia to help you. Make a poster of three animals that you are recommending. Draw each animal. Write two sentences about why you chose that animal. Share your poster with the class.

10. Change It! Game

Play Change It! with a classmate.

- Player 1 says an animal sentence using a past-tense verb. For example: *The tiger jumped.*

- Player 2 changes the sentence to include a present-tense verb. For example: *The tiger jumps.*

- Play until each of you has made ten sentences.

Name_____

1. The Cook's Helper

In *Sophie's Special Cake,* Sophie bakes a cake with help from her Nanny. Do you like to cook? Do you help in the kitchen at home?

- Write one thing you like to do in the kitchen.
- Write the steps for this activity.
- Use sequence words: *first, next, then, finally.*

Tell a classmate what you like to do in the kitchen. Explain your steps in the correct sequence.

2. Family Quilt

Look at the picture on page 229 in *Thunder Cake.* There's a colorful quilt. A *quilt* is a blanket made from squares with different designs. Make a family quilt from paper.

- Cut a sheet of construction paper into as many squares as you have family members. Include extended family and pets if you wish.
- Think of a design for each member of your family. You can use letters, names, numbers, shapes, or patterns.
- Draw one design on each square.
- Arrange the squares on another sheet of construction paper. When you decide on the arrangement or pattern you want, glue on the squares to make a "quilt."

Show your quilt to a classmate. Explain the meaning of each square.

Name_____

3. Poem to a Storm

Storms can be very noisy. Write a poem about a noisy storm.

- Use words that sound like noises. For example: *rumble.*
- Write at least four phrases or sentences.
- Use exclamation marks for some noisy words.
- Write *very* noisy words in capital letters.

Read your poem to a classmate.

4. Storm Encounters

Have you ever experienced a storm? Write a personal narrative about what the storm was like and how you felt during it. Be sure to

- use personal pronouns like *I*, *we*, and *they*
- write about events in the order they happened

5. Rainy Day Fun

In *Thunder Cake,* the characters make a cake to entertain themselves during a storm. Imagine that your family is bored because it's raining. Think of ways to entertain them!

- Think of an activity your family can do indoors.
- Think of what your whole family likes to do.
- Then write how each family member can participate.

Share your ideas with your family.

Name_____

6. Me and Babushka

Patricia Polacco, the author of *Thunder Cake,* is of Russian and Ukrainian descent. In Russian, the word for Grandmother is *Babushka.* With a partner, write a play about visiting Babushka.

- One of you will be the character of Babushka and the other will be the visitor.

- Look at the pictures in *Thunder Cake*. Think of questions to ask Babushka.

Look at the play *Sun and Ice* on pages 258 through 261 to see the way plays are written. Then write your play on lined paper.

- Continue until you have six questions and answers.

- Present your play to a small group.

7. Sun and Ice

How is sun the same or different from ice?

- Use a chart like the one below.

- Brainstorm all the characteristics and weather words you can think of to describe sun and ice.

- Find more information about these two kinds of weather in an encyclopedia or a geography book.

Display your diagram on a classroom bulletin board.

Sun	Ice

Name _____

Phonics Library

8. *The Family Garden*

Reread the story *The Family Garden* and fill in a story map about what happens in the story. Be sure to include what happens at the beginning, middle, and end of the story.

9. My Favorite Season

Think of which season is your favorite and why. Make a poster of your favorite season.

- Draw the shapes and colors of the season.
- Draw a scene of yourself and your family or friends having fun outdoors during this season.
- Write a catchy title for your scene.

Bring your poster home to share with your family. Explain why this season is your favorite.

10. Acrostic Game

Play this weather word game with a classmate.

- Choose a weather word, such as *thunder.*
- Write the letters of the word in a column.
- Take turns writing a phrase about weather that begins with each letter. For example:

    Terrible blizzard
    Hot sun
- Continue to play the game with other weather words.

Name_____

1. Still Life

Look at the picture on page 295 of *The Art Lesson.* The children are painting a still life. A *still life* is a painting of objects. Make some still life groupings. Collect at least six objects. Group the objects on a table in an interesting way. Ask a classmate to join you to talk about your still life.

- Walk around the table and stop four times. Talk about how the still life looks each time.

- Give your opinion of which view is best for a painting.

Now each of you should draw the still life from your favorite view.

2. *-ING* Words

Play this word game with a classmate.

- One player points to a person in a picture in *The Art Lesson.*

- The other player tells what the person is doing. The player must say only one word and it must end in *-ing.*

- Take turns finding pictures and saying *-ing* words.

Name_____

On My
Way
Practice
Reader

3. *The Garden County Fair*

Create a time line of events in *The Garden County Fair.*

- Look at the pictures in the story.

- List the events of the fair in order.

- Make a time line of the events for the day on a poster.

You can add pictures to your time line if you wish.

4. Connect-a-Dot

Prepare an art game to play with a classmate.

- Draw an object on a sheet of paper.

- Place white tissue paper over the drawing.

- Use a marker to make a connect-a-dot picture. Dab dots along the lines of the drawing underneath.

- Number the dots, starting with the number 1.

Give your dot picture to a classmate. Tell your classmate to connect the dots by following the numbers.

5. Try This

Find solutions to the problems in *The Art Lesson.*

- Use a Problem/Solution chart.

- Look at the pictures on pages 302 and 303.

- On your chart, write the problem you see in each picture.

- Write your own solution.

Talk about the events in each picture with a classmate.

6. Word Search

Create a word search using art words from the story.

• Make a list of six words. For example: *brush*.

• Write the words on graph paper either left to right or top to bottom.

• Surround the words with other alphabet letters to hide them.

• Ask a classmate to find the six words.

7. Artist

Write a paragraph that tells what you think Tommy is feeling in one of the pictures on pages 316, 317, and 318. Use what you see in the picture and what you know from the story. Check to see that each of your sentences has a naming part and an action part. Then get together with a group of classmates who chose the same picture and compare what you wrote.

Name_____

8. Dear Miss Landers

Imagine that you are Tommy's friend. Write a letter to Tommy's teacher in *The Art Lesson.*

- Think about why Tommy was upset.

- Read pages 306 and 309 for help.

- Write a letter telling Miss Landers why Tommy wanted to use his box of crayons.

9. My Portrait

Draw a portrait of yourself.

- Draw a portrait that shows your talent.

- Get ideas from page 294 in *The Art Lesson.*

- You can look in a mirror as you draw, if you like.

Ask a classmate to guess what the portrait says about you.

10. Carmen Lomas Garza

You learned about Carmen Lomas Garza's paintings. Look in art books or encyclopedias to find another one of her paintings. Write a paragraph describing the painting. Write about

- the colors used

- what you think the painting is about

- what you think the artist was trying to say

Name_____

1. My Performance

In the story *Sam Sings,* Sam was afraid to sing by himself on stage, even though he sang all the time. Think about a time that you were asked to perform or do something in front of a large group. Were you afraid like Sam? What did you finally do? Write a journal entry about that experience.

2. *The Garden County Fair*

Make a flyer to tell people about *The Garden Country Fair.*

- There are many different things to do at a fair. Make a list of the different activities to include in your flyer.

- Draw pictures of the different events.

- Remember to tell when and where the fair is.

- You may also find more information in an encyclopedia.

Share your flyer with a classmate. Ask them what events they would like to go to at the fair.

3. *The Garden County Fair/ Annie's Gifts*

Read *The Garden County Fair* or *Annie's Gifts.* Write a short summary about the story:

- Tell about the characters and the setting.

- Describe the main story events.

- Write about the talent of the main character.

Retell the story in your own words to a classmate.

Name _____

4. Sound Experiment

In *Moses Goes to a Concert,* you read about musical instruments. Conduct this sound experiment with a classmate.

- Find a book with a hard cover.
- Stretch a rubber band around the book, down the middle.
- Put two pencils under the band, one at each end.
- Pluck the band to make a sound.
- Try moving the pencils closer together. Does the sound change?
- Try plucking the band with a pick. Use a flat object. Does the sound change?

Now, write a paragraph telling what you learned about changes in sound.

5. Vowel Scene

- Draw a scene that contains four or five things with a long *i* sound, such as in *kite.*
- Next to each of those things write blanks for each letter in its name. For example, you would write __ __ __ __ by the picture of the kite. Write the words on the back of your paper.
- Trade scenes with a classmate. Each of you should try to fill in each other's picture. If you cannot tell what the picture is, ask your classmates for a clue.

Name _____

6. My Trip to a Concert

Have you ever been to a music concert? Write a short story about that experience. In your story, include

- who performed the concert and what type of music you heard

- when and where it was and whom you went with

- if you liked or disliked it and why

7. Shake It!

Make an instrument.

- Use a plastic cup as the container.

- Decide what to put inside. Choose a small, hard object.

- After you choose the kind of object, put some of them in the cup.

- Cut a circle from poster paper to fit the top of the cup. Tape it to the top.

Get together with some classmates. Sing a song together as you shake your instruments.

Name_____

8. Sign It

Look at the pictures of Moses and Ms. Elwyn using sign language in *Moses Goes to a Concert.* Create new sentences in sign language.

- First, write two sentences using words from the pictures.
- Then look for each word's sign. Practice signing the complete sentence.
- Sign the sentences for a classmate. Ask your classmate to guess the words as you sign.

9. Concert Tips

In the article "Go to a Concert," the author gives you tips on what to do at concerts. Make a poster that lists these tips. Draw pictures to go with the tips. Tell what kind of concert each tip is for. Share your poster with the class.

10. Music Survey

Who is everyone's favorite musical performer? Take a survey.

- Make a chart with three columns. Label the columns: *Student, Favorite Performer,* and *Details.*
- Ask classmates to name their favorite performer.
- Write the students' names in the first column.
- Write the performers' names in the second column.
- Write why they like the performer in the third column.
- Count the favorites and share the results.

1. What Happened?

Make a list of all the events that happened in the story *Mr. Mell Goes to Camp.* Then put the events in the order that they happened. Compare lists with a classmate.

Phonics Library

2. *Will Holly Sing?*

At the end of the story *Will Holly Sing?*, Holly sings a song called "Good Friends" and dedicates it to Tom and Luke. Why does she do this? Write a short paragraph explaining Holly's choice.

3. Questions Game

Play this game with a classmate.

- Look through *The School Mural* to find illustrations.

- One player asks a question about the illustration.

- The other player answers the question.

Take turns asking questions. Check the answers by reading under each picture.

4. Planning a Project

Before the children in the class decided on their project in *The School Mural,* they had to plan. List the steps the children took to plan their project.

- Write down what Mrs. Sanchez asked the children to do.

- How did they decide on the project?

- Who helped them find a place to draw the mural?

- Look at Chapters 1, 2, and 3 for help.

- Remember to use *First, Next, Then,* and *Last.*

5. Illustrator

In *The School Mural,* children drew pictures of their school and community. Draw a picture of your school for a newspaper.

- Look around the room. Do you see something that would tell people about your school? For example: *a picture by a classmate, a classmate's clothes, an object on the teacher's desk.*

- Choose one thing for a picture in a news story. Draw it.

- Think of a catchy heading. Write it above the picture.

- Write a one-sentence caption under the picture.

Show your news picture to classmates.

6. Family Talent

What kind of talents does everyone have in your family?

- Make a web of your family and pets. In the center circle write *Family Talents.*

- Write one talent in the web for each family member. Include yourself.

Show the web to a classmate. Tell your classmate to ask questions about it.

7. It's Raining Inside!

Look at the *School Comics* on page 396. Can you help solve the problems? Make a *Solving Problems* chart like the one on page 197 in your Practice Book. Do these things for each problem:

- Write the problem in the first column.

- Think about as many ideas to solve the problem as you can. Write them down in the second column.

- Put the solution in the third column.

Share your solutions with a classmate. See if you have some of the same solutions.

Name _____

8. Compare

Look at the mural on pages 390-391 in *The School Mural*. Work with a classmate to compare the things in the mural.

- Compare two things. Use words that end in *-er*.

- Then compare three things. Use words that end in *-est*.

9. School Murals

Do you have ideas for murals in your school?

- Choose a place in your school for a mural.

- Make a web for and write ideas for murals in the webs.

- Draw a sketch of your mural.

Share your ideas with a classmate. Talk about how the mural will make a place interesting.

10. Hobbies

In the story, *The School Mural,* some of the children liked painting so much that it became their new hobby. What are some of your hobbies? Draw a picture of your favorite hobby. Under the picture write one or two sentences telling what the hobby is and why you like it. Share your drawing with a classmate.

Web

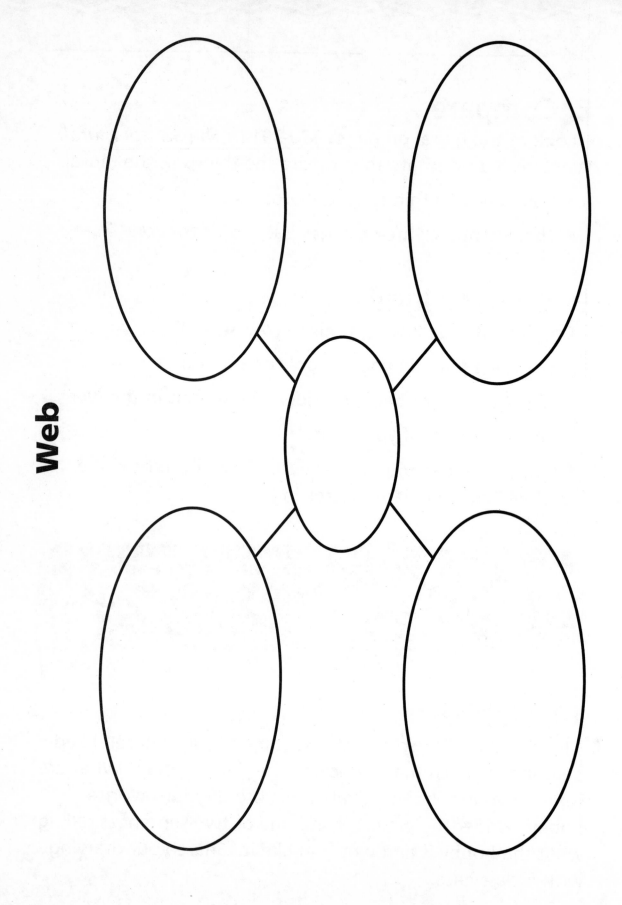

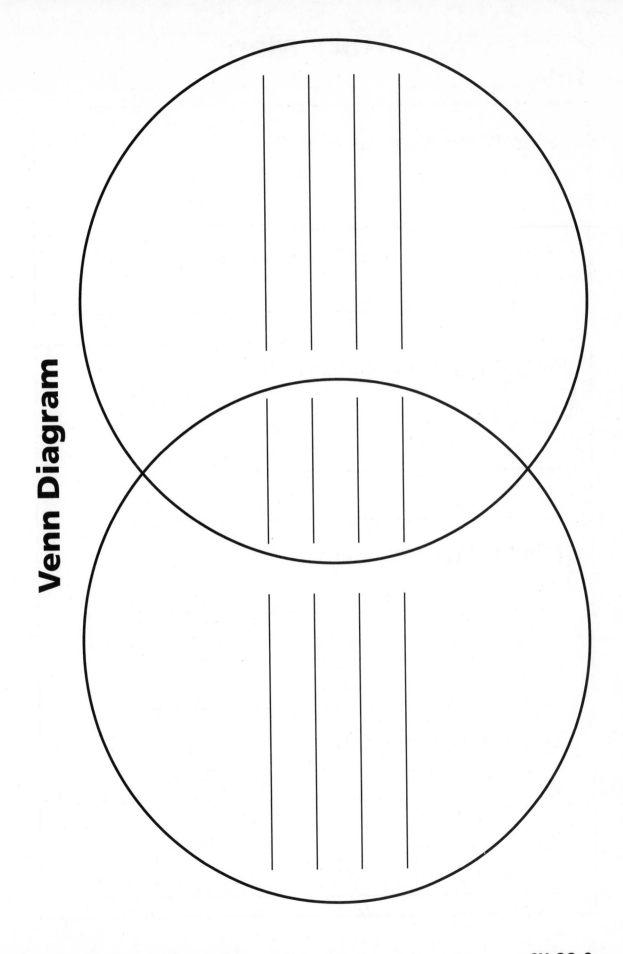

Venn Diagram

Story Map

Title:_____

Who (Who is in the story?)

_____

Where (Where does the story take place?)

_____

Beginning (What happens?)

_____

_____

_____

Middle (What happens?)

_____

_____

_____

End (What happens?)

_____

_____

_____

Grade 2 Graphic Organizer Master 3

K-W-L Chart

What I Know	What I Want to Learn	What I Learned

Grade 2 Graphic Organizer Master 4

Inference Chart

Story:_____

What the Character Is Like	Story Clues
_____	_____
_____	_____
_____	_____
_____	_____
_____	_____
_____	_____
_____	_____
_____	_____
_____	_____
_____	_____
_____	_____
_____	_____

Problem/Solution Chart

Problem	Ideas	Solution
_____	Page:_____	_____
_____	1._____	_____
_____	2._____	_____
_____	3._____	_____
_____	4._____	_____
_____	_____	_____
_____	_____	_____
_____	Page:_____	_____
_____	1._____	_____
_____	_____	_____
_____	2._____	_____
_____	_____	_____
_____	3._____	_____
_____	_____	_____

Cause and Effect Chart

Cause (Why does it happen?)		Effect (What happens?)
_____ _____ _____	→	_____ _____ _____
_____ _____ _____	→	_____ _____ _____
_____ _____ _____	→	_____ _____ _____
_____ _____ _____	→	_____ _____ _____
_____ _____ _____	→	_____ _____ _____

Grade 2 Graphic Organizer Master 7

Sequence of Events

First	
Next	
Last	

Copyright © Houghton Mifflin Company. All rights reserved.

Fantasy/Realism Chart

Could Not Really Happen	Could Really Happen
_____	_____
_____	_____
_____	_____
_____	_____
_____	_____
_____	_____
_____	_____
_____	_____
_____	_____
_____	_____
_____	_____
_____	_____
_____	_____

Grade 2 Graphic Organizer Master 9

Noting Details Chart

Details Chart

Statement: _____

_____

Page: _____ **Details:** _____

_____

_____

Statement: _____

_____

Page: _____ **Details:** _____

_____

_____

Statement: _____

_____

Page: _____ **Details:** _____

_____

_____

Management Profile

Room

☐ Arrangement

What do I need to improve the class for grouping and for independent centers?
Where can I post important objectives, confidence-building notices, and procedures?
Are there visibility issues? Floor space, wall space, shelf space, bulletin boards
Notes:

☐ Storage

What storage improvements can I make for students and myself?

_____

☐ Safety

Are there safety issues for any or all students?

Procedures

☐ Materials

Storage, distribution, putting away—how will I direct these?

_____

☐ Roll call/attendance

Is there a way to get an accurate record without taking so much time?

_____

☐ Bathroom, drinking fountain, office, library

What rules are in place and familiar to students? What might need special attention?

_____

☐ Cafeteria

How can I save time before and after to keep students focused?

_____

☐ Recess

What school policies need to be reiterated? When are the time drains?

_____

☐ Asking for help

How do I want students to ask questions? Do students know when and how they can
approach me? Have I made it clear how they can bring personal issues to my attention?

Transitions

☐ Arrival at school and in the classroom

What directions are needed?

_____

☐ Leaving the room and coming back

Should I try different strategies? Who can help me model this behavior?

☐ When the last bell rings

What do I need to cover beforehand to be ready?

_____

Group Work Form

Our names:

_____   _____   _____

_____   _____   _____

Activity title:

_____

What our group did:

_____

_____

_____

Does one of these descriptions fit how you worked together?
[Check one]

☐ We listened well to each other, and each of us did our part.
We finished the activity successfully.

☐ Sometimes we listened well to each other. We stayed on
task most of the time.

☐ We had trouble figuring out what we should do. We did
not complete the activity.

What might you do differently next time?

_____

_____

_____

_____

Checklist for Assessing Independence

Name   Date

- ☐ Listens to others in groups, waits turn, does not interrupt

- ☐ Participates fully in groups

- ☐ Supports group members' ideas

- ☐ Stays engaged and on-task during group work

- ☐ Completes assigned group task

Observations

_____

_____

_____

_____

_____

_____

_____

_____

_____

What I Can Do

Read a book silently in my seat.

Write a letter to describe what I've learned today.

Write in my journal.

Complete today's assignments.

Begin my homework assignments.

Work quietly on my project or activity.